PROMOTING WELFARE?

In memory of Harold White, Marjorie White and Kay Leonard

PROMOTING WELFARE?

Government information policy and social citizenship

Penny Leonard

First published in Great Britain in October 2003 by

The Policy Press
University of Bristol
Fourth Floor
Beacon House
Queen's Road
Bristol BS8 1QU
UK

Tel +44 (0)117 331 4054
Fax +44 (0)117 331 4093
e-mail tpp-info@bristol.ac.uk
www.policypress.org.uk

British Library Cataloguing in Publication Data

A catalogue record for this book is available from the British Library

ISBN 1 86134 488 0 hardback

A paperback version of this book is also available

Penny Leonard is an independent social researcher

Cover design by Qube Design Associates, Bristol.
Printed and bound in Great Britain by Hobbs the Printers Ltd, Southampton.

Contents

Foreword

This volume by Penny Leonard is a critical account of a research study into the relationship between information and citizenship. There are, it seems to me, three dimensions in which this book adds to the literature on citizenship and the welfare state and extends our understanding.

In the first place, Penny Leonard's study explores the contours of active citizenship – viewing citizenship not simply as a set of rights granted to the individual by the state but rather as an interactive concept. For her, citizenship is only fully achieved if citizens are empowered to participate in the definition of those rights and in their implementation.

Second, the study carefully considers, making use of primary material provided by policy makers at all levels, professionals and citizens, the extent to which the prospect of active citizenship is enhanced, or diminished, by the availability, nature and scope of information about rights.

Third, the study considers the ways in which traditional 'Marshall-type' literature on citizen rights are deficient in the aspiration to create a rights-based welfare state. Traditionally, citizenship theorists had seen the achievement of citizenship as something dependent solely on government intervention in the economy and the social fabric of UK society.

Following the Second World War and the election of a Labour government in 1945, the Party set about creating a reasoned and moral case for social democracy, defined here as a set of political ideas that suggest that the goal of socialism is achievable through the means of parliamentary democracy. The chief architect of this case was the late Tony Crosland – initially an Oxford politics don and later a Labour politician. His arguments, made most cogently in *The future of socialism* (1956) and *The conservative enemy* (1952a), suggested that the creation, inter alia, of a post-war welfare state had civilised UK capitalism and had transformed it from a system that *required* social and economic inequality into one where the achievement of greater equality and social justice were both desirable and possible:

> … while capitalism has not collapsed as a result of internal contradictions, it is possible to see a transformation of capitalism occurring. Since 1945, capitalism has been undergoing a metamorphosis into a different system. (Crosland, 1952b, p 34)

It is clear, then, that for Crosland, and for the Labour Party that largely accepted his revision of its earlier adherence to a more overt class analysis, the political project for post-war social democrats did not include the overthrow of capitalism! Capitalism had already tamed itself and the main concern of social democrats was to work within the framework of post-capitalist politics to ensure the maximum benefits of transformed capitalism for all citizens.

Crosland's views on the role and nature of a welfare state, and its position in a mixed economy, provide interesting reading. They do so because they represented a social democratic manifesto and rationale for welfarism: a justification for maintaining a centrally funded universalist welfare state; a rationale for the extension of that welfare state to provide more equality through consumption-oriented social policies rather than production-oriented economic policies; a refutation of right-wing prescriptions for less welfare; and a rebuttal of the aspirations of the left outside of the Labour Party for a marriage of economic and social policies intended to bring about equality of outcome rather than equality of opportunity.

What we have here is the most elegant formulation of what is currently considered 'old Labour' or social democratic values:

- although it does not see the welfare state as about creating equality, it does see it as about redistributing resources;
- it proposes the marriage of economic and social policy to rectify 'diswelfares';
- it sees the welfare state as providing citizens with a cushion of security.

Marshall, like other theoreticians in the so-called 'citizenship school', believed that un-supplemented markets caused severe insecurity and wide economic inequalities. In effect one section of the population, the lower paid, bear the costs of progress as capitalism develops while another section, the owners of capital, reap the benefits. Welfare states according to Marshall, in his inaugural lecture as Professor of Sociology at Cambridge, mitigate these tendencies. Or, to put it another way, the welfare state in the UK is seen as redressing the economic balance of power by giving equal social rights to all (Marshall, 1963). Social rights (a welfare state) like the civil and political rights that had preceded them were, according to Marshall, part of a rights-based entitlement. Social rights like civil and political rights confer citizenship on their recipients:

- The right to welfare (one of Marshall's social rights) is connected to full membership of the community for the individual. Here Marshall was reinforcing one of Tony Crosland's arguments about the role of welfare. The objective and outcome of state welfare is a sort of equality that comes, in Marshall's words "from full membership of the societal community" (1963, p 80). The right to welfare, in other words, confers on the citizen rights to be treated like all other citizens in relation to welfare and therefore bestows a sort of equality of regard.
- If all citizens are to be treated alike as far as their right to welfare is concerned, then the welfare state must be based on a framework of *universal social policies*.

The social democratic settlement was then, for Marshall, a settlement on a package of rights, "from the right to a modicum of economic welfare and security to the right to share to the full in the social heritage and to live the life of a civilised being according to the standards prevailing in the society" (Marshall,

1963, p 74). In providing these rights, of course, the state also made citizens stakeholders in and protectors of social democracy.

Also of note is the implication that more critical approaches, which have indicated, for example, the ethnicity, gender and disability blindness of earlier citizenship work, also fail. They do so because they under-emphasise the role that information plays in the search for full citizenship.

Penny Leonard's book draws our attention to the fundamental conclusions that without an appropriate emphasis on, and theorisation of, the interaction between information and citizenship, the nature, shape, contours and success of the search for full citizenship are diminished.

References

Crosland, C.A.R. (1952a) *The conservative enemy*, London: Cape.

Crosland, C.A.R. (1952b) 'The transformation of capitalism', in R.H. Crossman (ed) *New Fabian essays*, London: Turnstile Press, p 34.

Crosland, C.A.R. (1956) *The future of socialism*, London: Cape.

Marshall, T.H. (1963) 'Citizenship and social class', in *Sociology at the crossroads*, London: Allen and Unwin.

Professor Michael Sullivan
Swansea, August 2003

Preface

The original idea for this book can be traced back to the many years I spent working in an information and advice agency. Every day, people were seeking information and on every conceivable topic: some knew exactly what they were looking for while others were unsure what there was to know, or unaware that information could be helpful to them at that time.

Although there appears to be a wealth of public information, it is evident on closer inspection that some government departments and agencies are keener than others to tell the public of available services. In addition, public information about the services that are provided may not be consistent within a department. It is also evident that information designed for the public comes in a variety of forms. For example, leaflets can be bright, well-designed and eye-catching to encourage the reader; but they can also be dull and dreary with closely printed text that makes any reader feel weary before beginning. On some subjects there is no easily available information. Consequently, many people do not have easy access to information about services and benefits to which they are entitled, and how they might qualify for them. Research over many years has shown consistently that it is this ignorance that prevents many people from claiming their entitlements.

This book explores the ways in which governments promote welfare and inform the public of their social rights as citizens. In doing so, it aims to redress the balance in research which has often concentrated on individual reasons for not claiming entitlements. The main purpose of the book is to use government information policy to analyse attitudes to citizenship.

The research was undertaken between 1997 and 2000. In order to understand how decisions about information provision were taken, I conducted a number of interviews with both current and retired policy makers. These were politicians with a particular interest or experience in the subject and senior government officials directly involved in information policy. Officers of both voluntary organisations and local authorities with relevant experience and knowledge were also interviewed. Their views give a valuable balance and alternative perspective to the 'official' line. I am grateful to them all for agreeing to talk to me about their work. Their interest in the subject matter of this book confirmed my belief that this was a worthwhile project. All those interviewed remain anonymous here and every effort has been made to obtain permission from each to use the material in this book.

Thanks are also due to my colleagues in the former Department of Social Policy at the University of Wales in Swansea. Ken Blakemore was particularly generous with his time, encouragement and guidance. And finally, this book would not have been completed without the steadfast and loving support of Andrew, Meg, Martin and Kait.

Penny Leonard
March 2003

List of abbreviations

BA	Benefits Agency
CPAG	Child Poverty Action Group
DHSS	Department of Health and Social Security
DLA	Disability Living Allowance
DSS	Department of Social Security
DWP	Department for Work and Pensions
FC	Family Credit
FIS	Family Income Supplement
IR	Inland Revenue
IS	Income Support
MIG	Minimum Income Guarantee
MPNI	Ministry of Pensions and National Insurance
MSS	Ministry of Social Security
NA	National Assistance
NAB	National Assistance Board
NACAB	National Association of Citizens' Advice Bureaux
NAO	National Audit Office
PRO	Public Record Office
SB	Supplementary Benefit
SBC	Supplementary Benefit Commission
SERPS	State Earnings Related Pension Scheme
SSAC	Social Security Advisory Committee
SSC	Social Security Committee
WFTC	Working Families Tax Credit

ONE

Introduction

Citizenship is a hollow concept if people do not also have access to information. (Steele, 1991, p 47)

To play our part as citizens by participating in society and by fulfilling both the rights and responsibilities of that status, we all need information. Citizenship is a concept which, by definition, aims to be inclusive, and which implies at least some sort of equality and a common shared feeling of belonging. It would seem to follow that information should be available equally to all citizens, and on each of those subjects about which we need to be informed in order to function effectively as citizens. Information is essential for each component of citizenship: civil, political and social. We expect that information to be comprehensive, consistent, accurate and universal. Anything less would deny at least some, if not all, aspects of citizenship for those who are not fully informed or who are misinformed. That would seem to contradict both the basis on which citizenship is 'bestowed' (Marshall, 1963) and the values underpinning the postwar social democratic welfare state.

However, this study of information (and the policies that determine its provision) exposes a different reality: information provision is patchy. There appears to be no coherent policy. Practice varies greatly in scale. At one end of the scale are intensive (and expensive) national campaigns that focus on a particular service or benefit (such as the 'Right to Buy' publicity campaign, which resulted from the 1980 Housing Act and the Working Families Tax Credit campaign in 1999, for example). At the other is a virtual or complete absence of information available to the public on some other services or benefits (such as education benefits and Severe Hardship Payments for 16- to 17-year-olds). The evidence indicates that policy makers and providers of information make conscious decisions about the purpose, extent, nature and cost of that information. Information about welfare services and benefits, therefore, is not available equally to all those who are entitled to them. The corollary is that the services and benefits themselves are not available equally, either. The 'information poor' are a minority group that suffer from indirect (if not direct) discrimination in not being provided with information appropriate to their needs.

Much social policy research has thus far discussed problems and inequalities in access to information from the perspective of the service user or the disadvantaged group (see, for example, Bloch, 1993; Tinker et al, 1993; Moore, 1995; Vincent et al, 1995). This book, however, will focus on *policies* governing information provision. A concern that information should be comprehensive and accessible may overlook or fail to consider that, in practice, decisions are taken to actively publicise and promote some services and benefits but not others. Information policies that either deliberately or unintentionally provide or limit information will in turn necessarily affect access to those services and the level of use. They can result in high and low levels of take-up. Linking information policy to rights – that is, access to welfare services by potential users – has received little attention, but that is what this book aims to do.

This introductory chapter explains the link between citizenship and information and places the study in the context of the 'risk society', the policy-making process and power relations. It sets out the scope of the book before describing the overall approach and outline of the study.

Why citizenship and information?

Abel-Smith (1958) compared the position of the citizen with rights to welfare services to the consumer targeted by the market:

> No housewife alive in Britain today can be unaware of the claimed merits of 'Tide' – how to buy it and where to buy it, how to use it and how not to use it. But how many housewives know how to change their doctor, how to summon the National Assistance Board Officer, or what welfare services are available and how to get them? Why is the consumer always right and the citizen usually wrong? (Abel-Smith, 1958, p 67)

'Tide' is a long-forgotten commodity, no longer available on grocers' shelves, but housewives (and everyone else for that matter), being citizens, still need information in order to change their doctor, to claim welfare services or benefits, as well as to exercise their choice as consumers. Effective publicity in the marketplace, then as now, is not matched by the effort to inform citizens about their social rights. A measure of the commitment to citizenship rights would be demonstrated by equal access for all to welfare services and benefits. This commitment is called into question when there is a lack of effective information.

It seemed natural that the concept of citizenship should underpin this study. Although there are undoubtedly problems with the concept, it is an attempt at least to regard all 'citizens' as of equal worth in some way. It defines the relationship between individuals and the state. It is a contested and changing concept according to differing political perspectives, traditions and definitions, both within government and without. It is a concept that requires constant reappraisal, as it has since Marshall's seminal lecture of 1949 (Marshall, 1963). However, the notion of citizenship has regained prominence in political and academic discourse over the last decade or so (Coote, 1992; Kymlicka and Norman, 1994; Rees, 1995a; Greenaway, 1998; Dean, 1999). There have been attempts to redefine it so that the concept is more relevant to a multicultural, diverse and inclusive society (Taylor, 1989; Bulmer and Rees, 1996; Lister, 1997; Wilson, 1997).

Citizenship is also a useful concept for this study since it is often cited as justification for the existence of the welfare state, conferring rights to services and benefits (King and Waldron, 1988; Turner, 1990). Debate about the future of the welfare state, especially since the fracturing of the postwar consensus by the early 1980s (Sullivan, 1996), continues to cause uncertainty.

There is also uncertainty among politicians about how to resolve the many and often contradictory issues involved in making policy. In the absence of a complete overhaul of welfare, complexity seems to be an inevitable consequence of incremental changes in policy and practice. This has profound implications for any government committed to informing citizens about their rights. The idea of the 'information society' has attracted more general interest, in particular in relation to new technology. This has raised wider questions about the nature and status of information, the potential for service delivery and methods of information dissemination (Poster, 1990; Hughes and Moore, 1993; Steele, 1997).

The risk society

Uncertainty about what welfare services and benefits are currently available, and about what can be expected in the future, is part of the debate about the developing nature and status of citizenship. In the 'risk society', information is a key factor in enabling citizens to understand their rights. Postwar legislation in the late 1940s introduced services and financial assistance to help meet risks encountered by all citizens at some time from 'the cradle to the grave'. One of the tasks for information providers, especially in the early years of the welfare state, was to get the message across to the public that everyone could trust and depend on those services in time of need. Although the scope and function of those services has changed, the role of the welfare state continued for the most part to be largely perceived as something to be relied upon by citizens for several decades. Financial assistance, for example, was expected to provide either a return for contributions or a 'safety net' when there were no other available resources.

By the end of the 20th century, much of that certainty had gone. The wider global economic and social context, as well as the changing perceptions of the role of state welfare by each of Britain's two main political parties, have left citizens anxious about the future and what they can expect from the state:

> The retreat of the welfare state is compounded by a new uncertainty about exactly who can be trusted to meet the needs that people may experience now or in the future ... the retreat of state welfare in coverage and also in terms of the quality of provision is much publicised, leading to apprehension that one of the major mechanisms for managing insecurity is no longer available. (Taylor-Gooby, 2000, p 9)

That apprehension may be felt, for example, by the increasing number of older people. The limited budgets of local authorities providing domiciliary care and the closure of many privately run residential and nursing homes raise questions about how older people's needs will be met in the future.

Uncertainty also applies to social security policy. A working lifetime of paying National Insurance contributions is no longer sufficient to ensure even a minimum income in retirement. Current information about benefits cannot be relied upon to be accurate about 'rights' in ten, 20 or 50 years' time. Apprehension and uncertainty heighten the importance of understanding how policies are made about what information to provide, and to whom.

Policy making and power

There is evidently a lack of coherent policy on information, especially information about the rights of citizenship (Steele, 1996). Furthermore, there are many interpretations of what is meant by 'policy'. Helpful definitions for this study include what people do, a "pattern of activity" which includes routines (Colebatch, 1998, p 89), and "anything which guides, constrains or limits actions" (Barrett and Fudge, 1981, p 273). The extent and purpose of government expenditure provides another useful approach (Levin, 1997). A lack of information, or inaction (Heclo, 1972) – be it the result of inertia or of deliberate decision – and situations in which the provision of information is not even on the agenda, have also to be understood as policy (Parry and Morriss, 1974).

The difficulty of trying to define and understand what is meant by 'policy' is matched by an increasing recognition that making policy is not a straightforward process. It results from a multiplicity of complex and dynamic processes and influences that sometimes conflict with one another (Marinetto, 1999). Policy making cannot be understood, therefore, according to traditional distinctions between rationalistic and incremental models. Nor is it helpful to regard it as a linear progression from a stated aim to a separate and distinct process of implementation.

There is an additional complication for information policy: it is contingent. It depends for its existence on those social policies about which it provides, or withholds, information. The rationale of those social policies themselves is likely to determine or influence the purpose and extent of information policy and practice. The nature of those social policies – that is, whether they are new or incremental changes to existing policies, whether they are planned in advance or appear as a ministerial 'whim', and so on – will also affect the information policy process and scope for informing the public.

All of this results in "manifestly significant differences in the extent to which individual benefits systems are publicised" (Hill, 1990, p 96). Publicity may be the result of deliberately researched and planned campaigns or ad hoc activity responding to topical events. Or, indeed, policy may result in deliberate decisions not to provide information. Alternatively, publicity may result from accident, oversight or inertia, or perhaps from a bureaucratic information machine routinely rolling on and thus preserving the status quo.

Without a uniform policy on information it is perhaps not surprising that government information provision is patchy. With regard to welfare benefits, for example, over and above a basic level of information there are campaigns and publicity initiatives for some benefits but not for others. Legislation does not necessarily clarify the picture. The responsibility to provide information is sometimes explicit. The 1992 Education (Schools) Act, for example, places a duty on every school to provide prescribed information in a prescribed manner, "to assist parents in choosing schools for their children" (section 16), giving effect to a government commitment to the Parents' Charter. More often, any responsibility is discretionary and imprecise. The 1970 Chronically Sick and Disabled Persons Act (updated by the 1986 Disabled Persons [Services Consultation and Representation] Act) requires local authorities to ensure that disabled people receive information about services, "from time to time at such times and in such a manner as they consider it appropriate" (section 1.2.a). Those choices, made within limited and competing budgets, will reflect the underlying intentions and assumptions of the policy makers and official attitudes towards the rights of citizenship.

Policy making, as a way of mediating the relationship between the state and individuals, represents an exercise of power. Hill (1997) suggests that power may be more important to politicians than policies and "may be used to personal ends rather than try to solve problems in the way presumed in discussions of policy analysis" (1997, p 9). The theme of power, however, has wider significance for this study. Not only do "Citizenship rights operate within the context of power" (Taylor, 1996, p 150) but information itself is also about power, the power of the possessor and the powerlessness of the 'information poor'.

Information empowers; a lack of information disempowers. It also denies the status of citizenship in a system that relies on those who are eligible being well enough informed to claim their rights. Conditions of access to information are power relations. According to Taylor (1989, 1996) there is a "false universalism of state welfare" in which power relations exclude and marginalise some groups, limiting the extent to which the ideal of citizenship can be fulfilled. New technology (such as the Internet as a source of information) has the potential to alter the balance of power and the relationship between service providers and users. For example, many patients are now much better informed about their condition when visiting their GP than ever before. The themes of policy making and power have also however to be understood in the wider context of a traditional culture of secrecy (Steele, 1997).

The scope of this book

The central questions addressed by this book are: how far is information about welfare services and benefits provided to enable citizens to exercise their social rights, and how far is information policy governed by other considerations?

Finding the answers to these questions is an attempt to find plausible explanations for government information policy. Other questions arise in the course of doing so: What other possible explanations might determine policy about information provision? What are the underlying assumptions and intentions of those policies? Why is information provision so patchy when it is a prerequisite for exercising the social rights of citizenship?

The use of the concept of citizenship – that is, linking an understanding of rights with government provision of information – raises other issues addressed in the book. Do citizens have rights to information? Who is responsible for providing information? How proactive is government in information provision or, conversely, how active are citizens expected to be in finding out for themselves? To what degree, if any, are the 'information poor' responsible for their own ignorance and consequent failure to claim their entitlements?

To explore these questions, this book concentrates on social rights and on government information policies from 1948. The focus on government-provided information is not intended to deny the important contribution of other organisations in enabling people to access the services and benefits to which they are entitled. Indeed, some of their views are included in later chapters and provide an important perspective on the main questions addressed in this book. However, to include a detailed study of their contribution to informing the public would have distracted from the main thrust of this book: that is, linking information policy with government attitudes to citizenship and rights.

Social security policy has been chosen as the main focus for the book. Information to the public about other welfare state services equally could provide evidence to explore the link between information and citizenship. Similar questions to those mentioned earlier can be asked of information policy about personal social services, education, housing or health, for example. Although there are significant differences in their objectives, administration, levels of use and attitudes of both users and non-users, the approach and findings of this study can be applied more widely to other areas of welfare provision.

However, social security policy provides a particularly valuable focus. It occupies a central and influential place at the heart of the welfare state. Over half the population claim welfare benefits at any one time (DSS, 2000b). Around a third of government total managed expenditure (£104 billion) was spent on social security in 2000/2001 (*Social Trends*, 2002). In contrast to other welfare services, the sometimes ambivalent attitude of the public and the media towards claimants, and claimants' own attitudes to receiving 'benefit', would seem to place a particular onus on welfare benefit providers to inform. In this controversial area, government must also be clear in its objectives.

> The views of the government, its officials and members of the public on the extent to which specific welfare 'rights' exist will have a critical impact upon the 'take-up' of benefits. Many problems of access to benefit stem

> from a lack of social and political consensus about rights to state aid for deprived or dependent groups in the population. (Hill, 1976, p 74)

This book is not a challenge to the purpose, structure or adequacy of welfare benefits themselves (although without an adequate income it is difficult to exercise rights and responsibilities and participate fully as a citizen). It is an exploration of information policies about those benefits and of the extent to which the objectives of those policies are to enable people to claim their rights. In concentrating on social rights, the importance of information for citizens about their social responsibilities is not denied. Any examination of citizenship must necessarily include the relationship and shifting balance over time between rights and responsibilities (Roche, 1992; Jordan, 1998). The balance is discussed in this book by its attempts to answer the key questions listed earlier in this introduction.

Information about means-tested welfare benefits is central to this book (although examples of other benefits are given where they provide helpful evidence). The need for information is arguably greater for this group of benefits than for those universal and contributory benefits, such as child benefit and retirement pension, which have take-up rates approaching 100%, despite little active publicity (Lister, 1976; Golding and Middleton, 1982). Potential claimants of means-tested benefits are more likely to be deterred by issues of complexity and stigma than claimants of other benefits (Berthould et al, 1986; Fry and Stark, 1987; Craig, 1991), or of other less controversial services such as education and health. Effective publicity, then, is critical to increase rates of take-up.

The phrase 'take-up' is used throughout this book as a measure of the effectiveness of information policy. It is defined by the Department of Social Security (DSS) thus:

> Take-up compares the number of benefit recipients, or the total amount received, with the number who would be receiving, or the total amount that would be received, if everyone took up their full entitlement. (DSS, 2000c, p 116)

This book will be concerned mostly with the number of claimants (that is, 'caseload based') rather than the amount of money spent (that is, 'expenditure based').

Approach and outline

Chapter Two explains the use of the concept of citizenship as the theoretical framework. It explores its contested and changing nature. Using information provision as its focus, the chapter then considers the nature of social rights, whether information can itself be regarded as a right, and where the responsibility lies for its provision. Chapter Three looks at broader issues concerning information. It examines governments' attitudes towards information provision in a culture of secrecy, as well as the nature of information, sources for potential claimants, and the importance for information policy of an understanding of claiming behaviour. Chapters Four, Five and Six explore social democratic, New Right and New Labour information policy respectively. Within the wider context of social and economic policies, these chapters look for evidence of attitudes to the citizenship status of different groups of claimants. They compare the rhetoric of information policy with the reality of information provision and consider explanations for any disparities. Chapters Seven and Eight are case studies of publicity and information about particular welfare benefits: in-work benefits for low wage earners and means-tested benefits for older people respectively. Chapter Nine seeks answers to the central questions: How far does available information about welfare services and benefits enable citizens to exercise their social rights, and how far is information policy governed by other considerations? The chapter summarises the explanations for information policy and in analysing the findings it teases out the relationship between the provision of information and the exercise of the social rights of citizenship.

This book as a whole sets out to explore an issue that has profound implications for social policy and for those who are eligible for welfare benefits.

TWO

Citizenship

This study is based on the premise that information is necessary to exercise the social rights of citizenship. A lack of information, or 'information poverty', can result in a lack of access to (and denial of) those rights. This chapter provides the theoretical framework of this book. It argues that citizenship provides a valuable underlying concept for exploring the questions addressed here. It questions the nature of citizenship, the rights and responsibilities of both the state and its citizens, and explores the implications of these for information policy.

Citizenship is a contested and problematic concept and it is important to consider the difficulties it presents. However, more than any other major concept in social policy, citizenship highlights the central role of information for an individual's access to welfare. It is intrinsic to the concept that welfare state services, and by implication the information provided about them, are available to each and every person (subject to qualifying conditions). Other concepts, such as consumerism or paternalism, do not demand that information should be available to everyone about all benefits.

This chapter also asserts that social citizenship provides a justification for the welfare state and a yardstick by which to analyse and measure social policies. Other less inclusive arguments for welfare provision are concerned with deciding who is and who is not deserving, and in policies that legitimise targeting or selective information provision. These result in corresponding choices about who receives information, and risk creating 'information poverty'.

The distinction needs to be made early on between information about the rights and responsibilities of citizenship on the one hand, and information about the nature of citizenship itself on the other. This book is about the former. The latter – what it is to be a good citizen – is currently the focus of debate, especially within education policy. In 2002, citizenship became a compulsory curriculum subject in secondary schools.

The concept of citizenship

The concept of citizenship was devised as, and continues to be invoked in defence of, a feeling of shared identity and community. Although it remains a contested notion, citizenship is a mechanism for regarding all people as equal in a way which is unrelated to – and irrespective of – social and economic inequalities. Sullivan (1998, p 74) summarises Alfred Marshall's influential 19th-century hypothesis thus: "there is a kind of human equality associated with the concept of full membership of a community". It has its roots in liberalism with an emphasis on formal equality, an absence of coercion and political participation in the electoral process (Hughes, 1998). The status of citizenship is universal and inclusive.

T.H. Marshall's seminal lecture of 1949 provides an important starting point for contemporary discussion of the relevance of citizenship. He defines citizenship as "a status bestowed on all those who are full members of a community" (Marshall, 1963, p 87). As such it implies a sense of belonging, participation, identity and of having a share in the social heritage and life of a civilised community. Citizenship is a relationship between the individual and the state, characterised by both rights and responsibilities. For Marshall, the former have three equal elements or parts – political, civil and social – which originated separately over time. Social rights, according to Marshall, were incorporated in the 20th century in an attempt to resolve, to legitimate or to justify (at least partially) the contradictions between political equality and the economic inequalities of the market. Social rights were also necessary as a gesture towards the abatement of class inequality.

> All who possess the status are equal with respect to the rights and duties with which the status is endowed. (Marshall, 1963, p 87)

The concept of citizenship is used as a justification for the existence of the welfare state, by means of policies that aim to guarantee "a right to economic welfare and a share in the standards of living prevailing in society" (Golding and Middleton, 1982, p 81). The aim is to encourage participation in the life of the community through the availability and distribution of resources to those who would otherwise be unable to acquire or exercise this equality of status (Alcock, 1989; Roche, 1992; Cox, 1998).

> The argument we are making is for public provision of a minimum level of welfare as a universal entitlement, defining a threshold below which people will not be allowed to fall without diminishing their sense and their capacities of citizenship. (King and Waldron, 1988, p 436)

This argument for the importance of citizenship stresses that a sense of community can only be developed when there is equal access to welfare services such as education, health and income maintenance (Greenaway, 1998).

> Marshall's work was important therefore in providing a theoretical perspective on a broader and deeper conception of social membership as expressed through the idea of a welfare state being itself the embodiment of certain social rights and claims. Citizenship became a form of entitlement. (Turner, 1990, p 211)

Clearly, information about such entitlements is crucial for people to be able to enjoy the status of citizenship. In this book, entitlements refer to those services and benefits which the law says are available to those who meet the qualifying conditions. The relationship between rights/entitlements and perceptions of need is not straightforward. Differing views on what constitutes a legitimate need and how those needs should be met have been explored elsewhere (see, for example, Doyal and Gough, 1991). Information demystifies welfare systems for potential users and, in facilitating access, is consistent with the spirit of social citizenship. This argument does not deny that justifications for the welfare state other than citizenship also require information policies.

Counter arguments from 'New Right' thinkers (for example, Joseph and Sumption, 1979; Mead, 1986) have sought to emphasise individualism and a competitive market economy. From these perspectives, state provision of welfare services risks destroying a sense of community and shared responsibility.

> New Right theorists and politicians have sought to bring about a reversal in the post-1945 expansion of the public sector, as manifested primarily in the growth of the welfare state. New Right theorists are troubled by the welfare state for both economic and moral reasons. (King and Waldron, 1988, p 416)

A minimalist welfare state emphasises self-reliance, where citizens are not simply passive recipients of rights.

For the New Right, Marshall's concept of social citizenship does not therefore provide a justification for the universal welfare state. Challenges over the past 50 years to both definitions of citizenship and to the welfare state have failed, however, to destroy either (although both have changed and been redefined). In many important ways the welfare state remains intact despite attempts to erode it, especially since 1979 (Cochrane and Clarke, 1993). For King and Waldron (1988, p 417) this provides "an indication of the extent to which welfare provision is now conceived of as a core element of citizenship in Western society".

This book focuses on the rights of social citizenship, but, as was mentioned earlier, rights cannot be divorced from responsibilities. Information about the responsibilities or duties of citizens is also crucial to the enjoyment of that status. The responsibilities of citizenship were part of the explicit philosophy of the postwar welfare state. Beveridge (1942, p 170) explained:

> The plan is not one for giving to everybody something for nothing or without trouble, or something that will free the recipients for ever thereafter from personal responsibilities.

Marshall (1963, p 117) was equally clear:

> If citizenship is invoked in the defence of rights, the corresponding duties of citizenship cannot be ignored.

What is less clear, and alters with ever-changing political perspectives and interpretations, is the nature of both rights and responsibilities and the balance between them for individual citizens. Information about what is expected of citizens is, once again, crucial. Its relevance to this study of information policy is clear: shifts in that balance result at times in citizens being expected to take responsibility to find out for themselves about welfare services and benefits – that is, to be active citizens, rather than to rely on information being provided by an active government. Such assumptions about individuals' responsibilities to seek, find and use information for themselves affect policy makers' judgements and decisions about what to provide.

The citizen of the charters

The notion of the citizen as envisaged in government charters of the early 1990s had the potential to be very useful for this study, since this notion placed emphasis on providing information (Miller and Peroni, 1992; Deakin, 1994; Butcher, 1995). The Citizen's Charter was launched in 1991 by the Conservative Prime Minister, John Major. It appeared to promise a more explicit, structured and codified approach to rights and responsibilities, which was based on a perceived need to improve public services. Its commitment to information was explicit:

> Full accurate information should be readily available, in plain language, about what services are being provided. (Citizen's Charter, 1991, p 5)

Charters for many separate government departments and agencies followed. While not doubting that each charter genuinely was intended to improve services, Ling (1994) spotted the problem common to all attempts to inform people of their rights:

> It does not help all of those who are unaware that they are entitled to benefit, those who are unaware of the existence of the charter, those who do not understand it. (Ling, 1994, p 53)

There were more fundamental criticisms:

> The Charter concept has radical potential but this largely rests in the notion of citizenship and the rights and responsibilities it implies. The Citizen's Charter, however, is not a charter for citizens and there is absolutely no indication that it ever will be. (Wilson, 1996, p 60)

Wilson (1996) argues that the Citizen's Charter was part of an attempt to improve public services by reducing public sector activity and improving efficiency, among other things. Butcher (1995, p 152) agrees that charters are about responding to public services, and "not about enhancing peoples' rights as citizens".

Charters were criticised – and continue to be criticised – for treating citizens as individual consumers or users with choice. This approach is reminiscent of Abel-Smith's (1958) housewife cited in Chapter One, ignorant of her rights to welfare services and benefits. The comparison was made there with information based on market principles, individual freedom and self-interest. Although citizens and consumers have common information needs, "citizenship as consumerism" (Miller and Peroni, 1992, p 257) does not have any democratic basis. It is not an appropriate model for a feeling of shared belonging, or for the nature and distribution of welfare. A pilot project was launched in 1997 to introduce vouchers for nursery education, providing choice for service users and competition for providers. It was short-lived. The difficulty in obtaining information about remedies and the arbitrary nature of those remedies led Deakin (1994, p 53) to conclude that charters provide "no rights or fixed entitlements – merely concessions that can be withdrawn at will".

In contrast, social citizenship confers rights. It aims to mitigate the inequalities of the market and aims for an equality of status for all citizens. Providing information for citizens to decide whether or not to claim their rights is crucial, even though users of welfare services normally have little choice of provider, service or benefit. One senior official described the distinction this way:

> "I do have a slight problem talking about 'customers' when they haven't got a choice…. Somebody suggested that 'claimants' was demeaning. I don't have a problem with somebody claiming what they are entitled to, I'm quite happy with that…. 'Customer' implies to me some degree of choice: I can take my custom elsewhere if I'm not happy with the service that I receive, and obviously you can't with the Benefits Agency…. DSS has always continued to call our customers 'claimants'."

A contested and changing concept

Marshall did not intend that there be a definitive fixed meaning for 'citizenship' (King and Waldron, 1988). Rather, he saw it as a dynamic concept, a process in which the balance between, and nature of, rights and responsibilities would change over time. It has to adjust and be seen in context: "Changes in political regimes and agendas usually entail changes in the uses and meanings of citizenship" (Gunsteren, 1998, p 11). The social policies of different regimes are used to promote or to undermine citizenship.

Postwar social democratic consensus – based on the policies of Beveridge and theorising of Marshall (Lister, 1998b) – chimed with the public yearning for an inclusive and more equal society. The notion of citizenship fitted the bill. Over the years that followed, however, it can be said to have lost some of its salience and importance with the fracturing of the postwar consensus

(Sullivan, 1996; Powell and Hewitt, 1998). A variety of factors – political, economic and social – led to the compromising of, and concessions to, a universal welfare state available and accessible for all on equal terms and free at the point of use. These also cast doubt on the relevance of the concept of citizenship. During the 1990s, however, "citizenship has become the 'buzzword' among thinkers on all points of the political spectrum" (Kymlicka and Norman, 1994, p 352). Once again, it became more useful as a concept in academic and political discourse as a way of trying to understand the nature and purpose of the welfare state (Taylor, 1989; Coote, 1992; Lister, 1997; Dean, 1999). As a concept with a real impact on people's lives, citizenship also provides a useful measure of the effectiveness of social policies.

The current context is different from the postwar climate in which Marshall was writing. The real world has moved on. Changes in social structure, patterns of employment, welfare pluralism and recognising diversity pose challenges for the contemporary relevance of Marshall's definition. Citizenship needs to accommodate diversity unrecognised by Marshall or Beveridge, and which is not antithetical to a universality of status (Williams, 1999). These changes also affect the services and benefits that constitute the welfare state, and resulting information policy. Minority groups, for example, may have information needs that are not met by traditional methods of dissemination, while new technology offers the prospect of more diverse ways of informing. These changes do not necessarily invalidate or diminish the contemporary usefulness of the concept of citizenship. At its heart remains the relationship between the state and individuals.

Citizenship has provided and continues to provide a helpful model to understand the direction and purpose of welfare, to plan policies, and to compare with earlier schemes and schemes in other countries. It combines the rights and responsibilities for the delivery of welfare – including providing information – with the rights and responsibilities of individuals as users or recipients. This chapter now explores the validity and nature of social rights and assesses whether information itself can be regarded as a social right.

Social rights of citizenship

Debate continues across the political spectrum about the validity of Marshall's addition of social rights as equals to political and civil rights. In modern welfare states, there is "the contradiction between the conviction that services and benefits should be there as a right for those who need them, and a belief in the law of the market" (van Oorschot, 1991, p 17). Some argue that there is a growing wider acceptance of social rights, embodied in the welfare state:

> Collective provision of welfare is associated now with an idea of social citizenship, and is taken to be comparable in status and importance to other aspects of citizenship such as the right to own property and the right to vote

> … such welfare 'rights' are integral to the contemporary sense of citizenship. (King and Waldron, 1988, p 417)

> Over the past 20 years there has been growing acceptance of social security and allied benefits as rights to be claimed by entitled citizens, rather than as a personal favour from the government to the poor. (Berthould et al, 1986, p 1)

The New Right, however, regards social rights as lesser or inferior rights, if they are rights at all:

> the New Right asserts that only civil and political rights are genuine rights of citizenship whereas economic and social rights are not. (Plant, 1988a, p 11)

Mead (1986) does not reject the validity of rights, but argues that obligation rather than entitlement should be the basis of citizenship. From this perspective, unconditional welfare and social rights undermine morals and responsibility. This is a theme that has become more familiar over the last decade, in particular with changes to social security policy introduced by New Labour since 1997. According to Powell (2000, p 47) the validity of rights is part of a definition of citizenship which "moves from 'dutiless rights' towards 'conditional welfare'". There are clearly implications of this shift for government information policy that will be examined in later chapters.

Information as a right

Whatever the balance between social rights and duties, there seems little controversy about the need for information about them. "Indeed, if rights are to exist in a real sense, it is essential that those entitled to social services know what their rights are and that they are able to lay claim to them" (Barbalet, 1988, p 54).

However, this was not always the received view. The perceived dangers of information provision were recognised by the Ministry of Health in their Annual Report 1926/27. It resisted the publication of scale rates for Poor Law relief because of "a grave danger lest the recipients may begin to regard the gift as a right" (cited in de Schweinitz, 1961, p 212). However, Poor Law relief, unlike the postwar welfare state, was not based on a concept of social citizenship. Marshall (1963, p 84) described it as an alternative to citizenship, a "divorce of social rights from the status of citizenship". Recipients were stripped of their civil and political citizenship. Information, or common knowledge, about the harsh conditions for those claiming relief provided a potent deterrent to claiming.

The status of information – that is, whether it can be regarded as a right of social citizenship – will influence decisions about the provision of information. One politician interviewed for this study was clear in his view, asking: "Why should there be rights to information?" Barbalet (1988) regards social rights as 'facilitators' to enable the exercise of other rights, rather than rights in themselves as a constituent of citizenship:

> First, citizenship rights are rights of participation in a common national community. Social rights may be required for the practice of citizenship in so far as they enable such participation. But this is precisely to say that as a means of facilitating citizenship they cannot be said to constitute it. (Barbalet, 1988, p 67)

For Taylor, information is also a facilitator but not a right: "The meeting of need, implies not just a set of rights but the power to achieve needs, in terms of access to resources" (1989, p 27). Rees argues that such is the essential nature of rights: "all rights facilitate, civil and political ones included. Rights are like keys, which, if turned, may provide access to a building" (1995a, p 315).

Titmuss (1987, p 244) was clear about the importance of information:

> If a case is made for social rights, there's a need to help individuals to know their rights. Without information rights lose their efficacy. Social rights are essentially rights of access and recipience, not rights of action.

Moore and Steele (1991, p 2) echo his view:

> Increasingly it is being recognised that information is, in fact, an essential element of citizenship: without access to information people cannot play their full part as citizens, nor can they take advantage of the benefits which citizenship can offer.

The UN Centre for Human Rights in 1996 was more precise, regarding the "right to receive and impart information" as of "fundamental importance to the principles of equality of treatment" (UN, 1996, article 15). The National Consumer Council (NCC) is equally clear, regarding information as 'The Fourth Right of Citizenship': "Without the right to education and information the other three sets of rights are liable to be hollow shams" (NCC, 1977, p 6).

Similarly, Galligan (1992, p 64) adds a third right in making the link between substantive and procedural rights (the former referring to outcomes, the latter to access and treatment [Coote, 1992; Foster, 1983]):

> It is part of the very idea of a substantive right that procedures be available to secure it. In welfare this means that where there are rights to certain benefits, there are procedural rights to the means necessary to obtain those benefits.... Procedures are therefore needed to ensure that all citizens have access to information about services and procedures, with appropriate help for those who need it, to secure information, to utilize procedures, and to gain access to services.

Others share the view that information should be a right. One politician interviewed as part of this study put it this way:

> "Well, yes, I think so. I think government has a duty to promote its social policies and to inform people about duties and rights. A citizen has certain responsibilities and certain rights, and the rights to information are really rather important aren't they?"

Two senior officers of voluntary agencies were clear about the need for information but more equivocal about its status:

> "Yes, but I don't know what that would look like. I don't know how you would enshrine such a right except by imposing duties on departments to do x, y and z. And it's not just about providing, it's also about how and to whom and that sort of thing."

Also:

> "There is a basic right that information is there, but in terms of accessing that right it's the resources. Information must be a key right for us."

These last comments illustrate the difficulty of separating the concept of rights from the practicality of enabling people to exercise them. Some of these practical difficulties are raised as objections to the validity of rights per se. The issues of universality, conditionality, specificity, enforceability and resources are now discussed in turn. The questions asked here about information as a right apply equally to other rights – social, political and civil.

The need for information is not disputed; however, there is not agreement about whether needs provide a basis for rights. According to Taylor (1989), needs-based rights tend to be selective, whereas citizenship-based rights tend to be universal. Only citizenship-based rights fit with social democratic definitions of citizenship. Rights to welfare are 'universal' for those who meet the criteria or conditions. Alcock (1989) suggests that rights to universal welfare do not imply uniform services. Information provision, for example in minority languages and different formats, can address the wider problem of an inclusive and equal citizenship that is both diverse and dynamic. More recent debate about citizenship has sought a definition based on a 'differentiated universalism' (Lister, 1997), a concept which allows for diversity without rejecting the intrinsic universality of citizenship.

A related problem in regarding information as a right is that of conditionality: "Rights are not a proper matter for bargaining" (Marshall, 1963, p 116). If information is given reluctantly, or on certain conditions, or by discriminating between potential recipients, can it be said to be a right? Having to ask for information, for example to claim means-tested benefits, is seen by some as a form of social exclusion, threatening to the integrity of the self (Twine, 1994).

As a right of citizenship the availability of information has to be independent of behaviour or "character assessment" (Plant, 1992, p 16) in an entitlement society. Placing conditions on the provision of information would clearly contradict notions of universal citizenship.

Social rights – and responsibilities – have also been criticised for being unspecified (Plant, 1992). There are examples of specific rights to information, such as the 1992 Education (Schools) Act mentioned in Chapter One of this book. However, much legislation that places a duty to provide does not specify how that information is to be provided. The 1986 Social Security Act, for example, allows choices to be made by those responsible for providing information. It imposes a duty on local authorities to publicise housing benefit with

> such steps *as appear to them appropriate* for the purpose of securing that persons who may be entitled to housing benefit from the authority become aware that they may be entitled to it. (1986 Social Security Act, section 31.4; emphasis added)

Such vague duties create problems for the argument that genuine rights have to be enforceable. Some information policy based on legislation could, in theory, be enforced in a court of law. For example, there is a requirement on landlords under the 1980 Housing Act (section 41) to inform those tenants eligible to buy property of their right to do so. However, as was discussed previously, even where there is legislation it is too often unspecific and therefore unenforceable in practice. Plant (1992, p 26) does not regard this as a problem for rights per se:

> If the idea of rights is linked to the idea of enforceability, then Marshallian social rights are actually a bit of a sham, and in fact possibly rather a cruel deception.

A statutory duty to inform social security claimants of their eligibility would be enforceable, at least in theory; attempts to enshrine it in legislation, however, have failed so far.

Enforceable rights also require a commitment of resources. For example, landlords must find the resources to inform eligible tenants of their 'right to buy'. In the absence of such responsibilities, policy makers will make choices about how to expend their resources. A lack of money or administrative capacity is often thought of as a stumbling block to information provision. Barbalet (1988) regards rights that are resource-dependent as secondary rights of citizenship. The validity of resource arguments and how they affect choices made about information provision are issues discussed throughout this book.

In summary, how does information measure up as a substantive right of citizenship? In the absence of legislation, information about social rights is neither universal nor uniform in its coverage; it may be conditional, and it is seldom specified or enforceable. It is resource-dependent and policy makers make choices about the level of resources committed to its provision. However, there is no acid or cast-iron test to determine what constitutes a substantive right as opposed to a legal or abstract right. Many of these 'shortcomings' or difficulties also apply to political and civil rights – "Social and economic rights are not in fact categorically different from civil and political rights" (Plant, 1992, p 17). Furthermore, these 'shortcomings' do not necessarily deny the status of information as a right. These characteristics may be desirable but are not essential to the nature of a right. Information may seem, in practice, to fall short of the ideal, but other social rights also fall short. Conversely, resources or facilitators that enable people to exercise their rights can have some or all of the characteristics of rights.

The evidence is inconclusive. Information policy is a measure of government objectives for welfare policies and a measure of intention towards claimants as citizens. That is why it is important to understand the basis on which information policy is made. Weale (1983) argues, helpfully for this study, that the language of rights for potential claimants, even if those rights are not a reality, is important to give priority, force and status to social goals. Foster (1983) is similarly helpful in distinguishing rights from non-rights. Her practical perspective summarises both the problematic nature of rights and the problem from the perspective of the claimant. Where Foster uses the word 'benefit', the reader here could substitute the word 'information':

> In theory a benefit as of right should give an individual a stronger claim to help than a discretionary benefit, but in practice the distinction between these two types of benefit may become blurred. How benefits are actually rationed and the extent to which the state either promotes or attempts to restrict a particular benefit may be more significant in terms of claimants so-called 'welfare rights' than the legal basis of that benefit. (Foster, 1983, p 127)

Marshall (1981, p 96), writing about the distinction between legal rights and discretionary decisions, constructs a hierarchy of rights and expectations. It is also helpful to this discussion when applied to information since it emphasises both public and policy makers' perceptions of need. He describes in turn rights that are "precisely defined and legally enforceable", rights that are discretionary but are "in accordance with current policy", "legitimate expectations ... based upon the avowed aims of policy" (which may be subject to decisions based on administrative practices and priorities) and, finally, generally accepted standards or public assumptions. Each of these models is useful to the discussion of information as a right. They will be used again in considering where the responsibility for information lies.

Responsibility for information

It is important to distinguish between two separate aspects of responsibility stemming from – or complementary to – social rights. First, this study is based on the premise that any right places (or implies) a responsibility on some other person or agency to provide opportunities that make it possible to exercise that right. This 'correlative obligation' (Rees, 1995a) is explored here. Second, there is the question of how much responsibility there is on individuals as citizens to seek out information and find out for themselves about their entitlements. At one extreme of the continuum is an ideological perspective that believes that government should not interfere with the lives of its citizens. At the other extreme is the belief that government has a duty actively to inform (passive) citizens of their entitlements. Political perspectives differ in the optimum degree of 'interference'. These perspectives are related to, and result from, definitions of citizenship and are explored in this book through information policy.

An acceptance of a need for information at the very least implies that information has to be provided and that a responsibility lies with some other person or agency:

> The exercise of rights presupposes that individuals know what their rights are, and that institutions exist which enable people to enforce them. (Adler and du Feu, 1974, p 67)

Even if there is no right to information, it can still be argued that the possession of other substantive and procedural social rights, that legitimate expectations and accepted standards of service place a responsibility on some other to provide information to enable people to exercise those rights. Each of Marshall's models can be said to confer responsibility.

Many regard this as a government responsibility. The UN Committee on Economic, Social and Cultural Rights accepts that social rights have received less attention in the past than civil and political rights. It asserts that:

> The question is not whether these rights are basic human rights, but rather what entitlements they imply and the legal nature of the obligations of States to realize them. (UN, 1996, p 5)

Claimants often expect to be informed when they are entitled to a welfare benefit and have no doubt about where the responsibility lies:

> They argued that if [benefits] were a right then the government would work out some way of paying money to those eligible straight away. (Briggs and Rees, 1980, p 148)

A 79-year-old widow assumed that she did not need to inquire because "I've took it for granted that they give me what they know I'm entitled to" (quoted in Costigan et al, 1999, p 52). One welfare rights manager put it this way: "The responsibility for providing information should be with the DSS and BA. The Local Authority ought not to employ people like me to provide information". Hill (1976, p 65) agrees that government has a responsibility:

> If individuals are not made fully aware of benefits available the practical outcome, whatever the intention of officials, will be the denial of rights. Do not governments therefore, have an obligation to ensure that persons entitled to public benefits, or services know about them?

Government acceptance of the responsibility to provide information was explicit at the beginning of the welfare state. The National Association of Citizens' Advice Bureaux (NACAB), set up in 1939 to provide information and advice about war-related problems, requested central government funding in 1944. The Ministry of Health responded "that in the future the government was likely to undertake the explanation of legislation and regulations itself" (NACAB, nd, p 3). The Ministry did not want to shirk the responsibility and saw no role for other agencies.

> I do feel that the CAB would be wise to accept the principle that both government departments and local authorities must make their services known to the people and must not rely on others to do it. (Ministry of Health, 1945, in Marshall, 1967, p 170)

However, in the absence of a statutory duty to provide information, governments have at times sought to avoid that responsibility. At a time when a Conservative government held power, Berthould et al (1986, p 64) commented "the onus is left to people to ask for benefits rather than on the DHSS to identify potential claimants". This was in tune with a belief in individual self-reliance and independence. There is more recent evidence however of delegation, and of explicit requests for help. In a NACAB press release of 24 September 1997, the Secretary of State for Social Security in the New Labour government, Harriet Harman, was quoted as saying that she wanted to work in partnership with NACAB. At the same time, "The CAB service recognises the need for policies which will encourage citizens to actively use government information" (NACAB, 1997, p 3). The nature of any such 'cooperation' will influence the extent, nature and cost of the government's own provision.

In our 'risk society', the need for comprehensive and effective information has grown. As welfare systems grew incrementally – and continue so to grow – it has long been recognised that people did not know, and perhaps could not be expected to know, about their entitlements (Walker, 1982; Foster, 1983; Hill, 1990). There is a widely held expectation – or an implicit responsibility – that governments, as policy makers, providers and administrators of welfare services and benefits, will inform people about their rights. Citizenship is a relationship between the state and its citizens. It is reasonable to expect the state to provide information to enable people to fulfil that status. Diverse practices and the lack of formal duty to provide (apart from legislation which specifically places a duty to do so), or only a vague duty to inform, prompt the central questions addressed by this book. Understanding the basis of information policy is one way of understanding attitudes to rights and definitions of citizenship.

THREE

Information

This study of government information policy, as a way of exploring attitudes to and definitions of citizenship, started from the premise that information is a prerequisite for exercising the rights of citizenship. This chapter explores broad issues concerning information that affect policy making and, therefore, adds to an understanding of how decisions are taken about information provision.

It is important to be clear what is meant by 'information' in this book, since it is a word that can have different meanings for different groups and in different contexts. Information is an elusive concept. To try to define it raises questions of a philosophical and legal nature and highlights paradoxes about its common usage. Raab (1994, p 342) asks:

> What do you get when you get 'information'? What can you do with it? What else do you need to know, as a consumer or citizen? And who is to say what you need, or might merely want, to know?

There is the common assumption that information is available and costless (Strauss, 1977) but, as Steele (1996) maintains (and this study confirms), it is a resource which needs to be managed. In this book 'information' is generally used to mean any material or activity that brings to the public or individuals' attention the existence of services and benefits to which they may be entitled. In assessing what constitutes information, or what help is provided, models of information – giving reflect both perceived levels of need and categories of service provision. They range from 'raw' information (that is, not specific to individual circumstances) from a variety of sources, through guidance in looking at individual options for action, to representation or advocacy in pursuing claims. All may be loosely labelled 'information' and are included here.

This chapter begins by summarising why information policy was chosen as a way to understand attitudes towards – and definitions of – citizenship. It continues by considering governments' attitudes to information in a 'culture of secrecy' before discussing the nature of the concept and whether it can be considered a public good. In order to set the scene for the following chapters, the next sections consider sources of information and models of claiming behaviour.

Why information?

There are several reasons for choosing to study information policy as a way of assessing government attitudes to citizenship. These have been raised earlier but are summarised here.

1. Information about welfare services and benefits is necessary at some time for all citizens as potential claimants. It is important to enable people to claim their entitlements and also for those who are not eligible to understand why they do not qualify.
2. The 'information poor' are excluded or marginalised. They share some of the experiences and consequences of discrimination of other minority groups that can result in them being 'second-class' citizens, unable to exercise to the full their social rights and responsibilities.
3. The need for information places a responsibility on some other person or agency to make information available.
4. Policy makers choose what information to provide. Those choices reveal the underlying intentions of policy makers and their attitudes to – and definitions of – citizenship.
5. Power is attached to decisions about the provision or withholding of information.

Of course, information is not the only key to claiming and receiving entitlements. There are other barriers and difficulties which may be equally, or more, insuperable than a lack of information for some citizens wanting to exercise their rights (Hill, 1990; Craig, 1991; Corden, 1999). One of these barriers was expressed in the following way by a politician all too aware of the difficulties:

> "There's an argument that says that we should be stepping back here and saying maybe, that information, the lack of information and the problem that creates, because I do not deny that it's a problem, is a symptom of a deeper problem which is that legislation is too complicated."

Decisions about how to inform the public are particularly difficult when the service or system is complex. There is a fundamental difficulty in disseminating information that is sufficient but does not mislead, is comprehensive but intelligible, and at the same time does not 'dumb down'. The complex child-support scheme provides an example. Many absent parents were unlikely to be able to assess their own liability to child maintenance payments, and parents-with-care their entitlements, even with the information provided by the Child Support Agency when it was introduced in 1993 (Garnham and Knights, 1993). Attempts to simplify the formula have yet to be put into practice. The confusion and uncertainty for parents, and the difficulties for government information providers, have been compounded by often sensational media publicity.

The importance of other barriers to claiming is not denied in this book. Some of them are considered later in this chapter because they are often bound up with the need for information. Poster (1990, p 7) stresses, however, the contemporary and wider importance of information:

> Information is presented as the key to contemporary living and society is divided between the information rich and the information poor. The 'informed' individual is a new social ideal.

Attitudes to information

It is important for this study to consider the context in which governments' information policy is shaped. In the UK, there has traditionally been a widespread practice of withholding information. This is a culture where a good case has to be made for parting with information (Bochel and Bochel, 1998). Drewery and Butcher (1991, p 175) recognise an official resistance to information dissemination resulting in part from legislation, but

> the rest is embedded in British political culture, institutional conventions and in the understandings and habits of civil service behaviour.... The ethic of secrecy and confidentiality is one of the basic working assumptions.

Charter 88, an organisation which campaigns for 'the right to know', works for a change from "the emphasis in Britain [which is] firmly on non-disclosure ... the unnecessary cobwebs of secrecy" to "the presumption ... in favour of openness and disclosure" (Charter 88, 1992).

There is a difference, of course, between information available to the public about the workings of government and policy decisions, and information that enables people to claim the services and benefits to which they are entitled. The point made here is that a culture of secrecy easily spills over from one to the other. Comparisons with other countries illustrate differences from the UK's culture. In Norway, for instance, there is a national government policy on citizenship information. This includes as one of its objectives, "to provide every citizen with information on his or her rights, duties and opportunities" in a way which is "comprehensive, responsive to needs and active not reactive" (Steele, 1996, p 16). In Sweden, there is traditionally a more open information policy that goes hand-in-hand with a commitment to mitigate class and gender inequalities (Cochrane and Clarke, 1993). It is more likely that everyone not only receives their entitlements, but also has plentiful information and help to understand those entitlements. In contrast, Steele (1997, p 308) recognises in the UK

> a tradition in which the concept of citizenship information has received little priority, or indeed little recognition, from policy makers at a senior or strategic level nationally.

There are indications of change, prompted partly by (or perhaps coinciding with) action in the European Union: "Policies on information and communication in the public sector are being developed more widely now than ever before ... in the UK and in Europe" (Steele, 1996, p 15). In Europe, citizens are "benefiting from a steadily increasing range of rights of access to information" (Moore, 1994, p 22). The EC Report, *Building the European information society for us all* (EC, 1997) describes one aim of the information society as enabling individuals to participate and play a full part in their community by reducing the exclusion of disadvantaged groups. 'Citizens First' is a Europe-wide information campaign designed to raise public awareness of citizens' rights.

New initiatives and an awareness of the need for information policies in the UK are also the result of national pressures. Among the reasons suggested for this shift have been

> the prominence given by Government and opposition parties to standards and efficiency in the public services ... the increasing discussion of openness, accountability and participation in public life. (Steele, 1997, p 331)

An interest in rights to information follows on from the prominence given to the idea of citizenship in the early 1990s, making the link, as this book does, between the two. During the 1992 General Election campaign, each major political party had policies to promote their notion of citizenship.

The principles of the Conservative government's 1991 Citizen's Charter, as previously discussed, included information and openness (as well as setting standards, choice and consultation, courtesy and helpfulness, putting things right and value for money) (Deakin, 1994). For example, information became available for parents about schools' performance, for tenants about standards and performance of housing management in key areas such as repair times, and for social service users more 'reliable' information on how to get services (Citizen's Charter, 1991). Charters have focussed the attention of public service providers on the way in which they inform the public.

> Delivering services in accordance with these charter principles involves a significant commitment to providing information.... This includes information from public bodies on the nature and extent of services to be provided to consumers. (Steele, 1991, p 282)

However, goals and activity were to be limited. The 1992 Right to Information Bill, which did not become law, would "provide for individuals to be notified of the availability of benefits *in certain circumstances*" (emphasis added). The 1993 'Open Government' White Paper aimed to make information available about the workings of government, and to provide access to information held about individuals by public bodies. It might also be thought to encourage a culture of more openness. According to Raab (1994, p 340), however, the

Code of Practice which followed the White Paper aims to tip the balance in favour of disclosure and against secrecy. "[Although it] ... does not concede the principle that rights should be the rule and restrictions the exception...."

The Conservative government introduced the Code of Practice, 'Access to Government Information', in 1994. While not legally binding (Bochel and Bochel, 1998), the Code required publication of "full and, where possible, comparable information about what services are being provided" (Home Office, 1994, p 3, iv). The Department of Social Security (DSS), for example, produced a leaflet entitled *Open government* (OG1) in 1995 resulting from the Citizen's Charter and the Code of Practice, which explained how to apply for information from the department. The leaflet stated that information about social security benefits was already available to the public from the department and its agencies.

While in opposition, the Labour Party expressed its commitment to a Freedom of Information Act. Speaking on 25 March 1996, Tony Blair recognised a need for change and for legislation:

> The real problem at present [is] the government grants information when it wants to. What is needed is a change in culture and a statutory obligation to make it a duty to release information to the people who elect the government. There is still too much addiction to secrecy.... So the presumption is that information should be, rather than should not be, released. (Blair, 1996)

Once in office, New Labour's Cabinet Office produced 'Service First: The New Charter Programme' as part of the 'Better Government' initiative. It created a new legal basis for people's right to know about public services. For example, its principles of public service delivery included the line "Be open and communicate clearly and effectively in plain language, to help people using public services: and provide full information about services, their cost and how well they perform" (Cabinet Office, 1998, p 1).

The government published its draft Freedom of Information Bill on 24 May 1999 (Home Office, 1999). This fulfilled a Labour Party manifesto commitment and provided statutory rights of access to information held by public authorities. The focus is on information about the workings and decisions of public bodies and access to their records and internal documents. There is less about information for service users but, again, a change in culture would foster provision of information about services and benefits.

> This programme of constitutional reform aims to involve people more closely in the decisions which affect their lives. Giving people greater access to information is essential to the aim. This will radically transform the relationship between Government and citizens.... Legislation is not sufficient in itself: there needs to be a change of culture within the public sector and the Government is determined to bring about this change. (Home Office, 1999, part 1)

The act received the Royal Assent on 30 November 2000 and is being phased in over several years. It is important to this study because it seemed to accept the need for a change in attitude as well as legislation. However, the result is legislation that falls short of expectations and preserves much of the culture of secrecy earlier denounced by Blair. The measures neither match earlier rhetoric and promises nor satisfy those who believe in an open society (Gore, 1999). It also falls short of a duty to inform citizens of their entitlements.

Information: the concept

Attempts to understand changes in the 'culture' of information are complicated by the "ambivalence and complexity" of the 'mode' of information (Poster, 1990, p 13). The extent to which information can be neutral, objective and rational was an issue recognised by those postwar disseminators of information who were keen to foster positive public attitudes to the new welfare state. Prime Minister Attlee was concerned that to retain the wartime machinery of the Ministry of Information "would mean ... risking the allegation that the present Government would use the Ministry as a medium for Party propaganda" (Cabinet Committee on the Post-War Organisation of Government Publicity, cited in Lowe, 1990, p 178). A senior official confirmed that it remains a dilemma:

> "There is a line which is party political.... Sometimes it is not easy to know the exact point where that line falls.... We have to be very careful there is not a political message."

The bulk of the postwar publicity was initially 'uncontroversial' including, for example, how to register with an NHS doctor. However, there was also recognition within the Central Office of Information (which succeeded the Ministry) of another dilemma which would become familiar over the following decades. To publicise national insurance and national assistance, for example, could risk encouraging welfare dependency or, conversely, it could be a positive factor in removing anxieties, reducing ill health and therefore provide an incentive to work (Lowe, 1990).

Lowe (1990, p 179) also describes at that time "the government's information offensive as an unwarranted exercise in political education which assumed, somewhat arrogantly, that the man in Whitehall 'knew best'". Decisions made on paternalistic or value-laden 'political' grounds risk denying information to those potential claimants whose behaviour is not approved, or of promoting selected benefits. Discussing the contemporary social context in the 'new information age', Watson (1998, p 227) acknowledges the potentially divisive nature of information, the digital divide, and the intrinsic power relations:

> Society is now differentiated as much by information as by the old cleavages of production and consumption with more and more people excluded and

marginalised from informational networks…. Power is thus crucially linked
with information … creating distinctive cultures and a new map of inclusions
and exclusions.

Power and information are inextricably linked. Lukes' (1974) three dimensions
of power – overt, covert and latent – are all important to this study. Overt and
covert power are familiar features of policy making and central to the discussion
in this book. Information is constructed, presented and put into context by
the provider (Raab, 1994); therefore, the relationship is unequal. For example,
when government obtains information about non-payment of child support,
or overpayments of social security benefits, it can recover the money owed.
There is (usually) no such backdating mechanism for claimants who discover
they could have been in receipt of benefit had they been informed earlier of
their entitlement.

Lukes' third dimension is also important to this study. It insidiously shapes
people's preferences and can be seen to work at two levels in this context. First,
it imbues policy makers with organisational culture and values which are
manifest, for example, in what information will be provided and in chosen
methods of provision. It suggests that hegemonic ideological influences tend
towards preserving the status quo. This could mean continuing traditional
(even if ineffective) methods of disseminating information rather than making
radical changes. Second, latent power influences the expectations of those not
informed of their rights and who may not be aware that they are missing out.
They are conditioned to 'information poverty' and, therefore, too often do not
protest. Power, in capitalist society and according to this analysis, works in
ways that are contrary to the interests of those who are excluded (Hill, 1997).

Control of information is a power relationship. It results in decisions about
the purpose of information, about what to provide and what to withhold,
about the methods and extent of provision and about allocation of resources.
Those decisions have consequences for governments and for service users and
claimants alike.

Information as a public good

Seldon (1977, p 19) includes, in his list of public goods, "A not obvious but
important one is the production of knowledge and information". The status
of a public good has implications for those responsible for information policy
and for the purpose, extent, nature and cost of that provision. It has parallels
with the distinction made earlier between social citizens and the 'citizen
consumer'.

Information certainly has some of the characteristics of a common good. It
is not inherently exclusive. It is not a scarce resource, it is reusable and usable
by several people at the same time it can be freely reproduced (but has a limited
'shelf life'), and the provider retains it after dissemination (Hughes and Moore,

1993). To treat it like any other commodity is to ignore these particular characteristics.

Although information can be manipulated for different purposes whoever provides it, there are important differences between information as a public good and information for consumers in the market. Jones (1985) argues that it is a question of whose needs are being served and how, and of who has access to the information. Private goods – and in this context information as a commodity – target those who can afford to pay and have choice. For example, information about welfare services and benefits can be obtained for a fee from some solicitors, accountants and private consultants. Access to public goods – including information – is not limited by ability to pay. Information should be freely available to all those who have an interest in those services or might have an interest in the future: that is, most people at some point over a lifetime.

Information about public services must, therefore, be different. It needs to ensure it reaches its audience in order to fulfil its purpose of empowering and making sure people understand their rights (Moore and Steele, 1991). Seldon (1977, p 17) asserts that public goods are those functions that only the state can perform because

> they cannot be refused to people who refuse to pay, and who would otherwise have a 'free ride' if they were not required to pay. Public goods, to be produced at all, cannot therefore be produced in response to individual specification in the market: they must be financed collectively by the method known as taxation.

Moore agrees. He argues (nd, p 5) that market forces alone can never satisfy the real demand for information:

> The State has a responsibility, therefore, to finance the provision of public information and advice services that are free at the point of use.

Non-government agencies offering a free service of advice and information are too often woefully underfunded. Others agree that the marketplace is not likely to produce information about welfare services effectively and recognise an ongoing need for government policy and provision of information (Jones, 1985; Steele, 1991). One senior official with responsibility for information policy was clear that this can also be in the government's own interest:

> "I had felt for a long time that public information, good investment in public information, means that everybody wins, because if you get the message out there people get the information that they need, they know how to act on it, so when they actually interact with you they probably need to do it only once and they'll get it right first time. So there's a huge investment, it's in the organisation's interest as much as the individual's."

Therefore, to conclude that information is a public good is to argue that it has a distinctive nature and that the need for information about public services is best met by public provision as part of a coherent strategy.

The implicit responsibility on government to provide information to the public about welfare services and benefits has already been discussed in this book. However, in a government 'Listening to Britain' survey, "Twice as many people think the public sector is worse than the private sector in providing information" (Hetherington, 1998, p 3). A government survey on attitudes to public services further revealed:

> one of the public's biggest gripes is having to waste their time looking for information about services. Respondents said they wanted more regular, simple and accessible information. (Cabinet Office Press Release, 3 June 1998, 136/98)

Acknowledging the difficulty of the task, one politician observed:

> "There is I suppose another problem: quite what do you mean? Information is a good deal easier to define, but determining how it is made available, the ways in which it is to be imparted, is quite another matter. Quite what is it that you are talking about? Somewhere between prime-time television advertising every night and a small footnote that can only be read if you've got a magnifying glass!"

These comments serve to illustrate the connection between the status and purpose of public information and methods of provision. There is a variety of methods of provision, some long established, routine and traditional (for example, posters and leaflets), others innovative and which move with the times (for example, the Internet, or using data already available to contact individuals who may be eligible). Providers of information need to be aware of the implications and effectiveness of different methods of provision, both within the wider context of the issues discussed earlier as well as their affect on the likely outcome. They also need to understand how people make decisions about where to go for information.

Sources of information

Information policy makers need to understand people's preferences concerning where to go for information and to be aware of what other information providers have to offer.

Research has shown that there is a variety of available sources for claimants and potential claimants to receive information about their welfare benefit entitlements (Briggs and Rees, 1980; Perkins et al, 1991; Bloch, 1993; Vincent et al, 1995; Cummins, 1996). This may be confusing for potential claimants who do not know the 'right' or best place to seek information. Each source may complement or contradict one another. However, choice can also provide a necessary variety of ways of provision, organisational ethos, attitude and approach to the giving of information that enables more people to obtain information. Silverstein (1984, p 37) describes a process of information thus:

> Around every individual exists a formal and informal information network. The size and quality of the networks, however, may vary from one person to another.

How do people choose where to pick up relevant information? The way that people choose where to go for information is often complex and has implications for government information policy. Knowledge of likely sources is obviously a basic factor. Choice may then differ between existing users of services and potential – or first-time – users. Much depends on how much they already know, as well as on previous experience, ease of access (both physical and 'user friendliness'), the service or benefit about which information is sought, and the circumstances which have precipitated the search for information. Feelings of confusion will also affect individual choice and confidence about where to find information. Moore and Steele (1991, p 129), describing the complexity of information about the financial implications of moving into residential care, confirm uncertainty and ignorance about where to find information:

> People do not have much idea about where to go for help on these topics and make little use of formal information sources.

Lack of knowledge and uncertainty may combine to produce doubts about eligibility. Misunderstanding and confusion are exacerbated by the complexity of welfare services.

The choice of where to go for information includes:

- central government departments and agencies at national, regional and local offices;
- local authorities;
- voluntary sector organisations (such as Citizens' Advice Bureaux, law centres, independent information and advice centres);
- national and local single issue and self-help groups;
- other local community sources (GPs, health visitors, social workers and other professionals, faith communities, MPs and councillors);
- libraries, post offices and other locations for leaflets and posters;
- the media;
- informal contacts (family, friends, neighbours).

Contact may be made in person, by telephone, e-mail or letter, or by accessing a range of Internet sites and other new electronic channels (Hudson, 2002). With such an apparent wealth of possible sources, how important is government information provision? A survey for the DSS finds that "Customers gained information in a very haphazard way, mostly from friends and family and through chance encounters" (Vincent et al, 1995, p 71). A survey commissioned by the Benefits Agency (BA) concludes that "Sources of information on eligibility for benefits have changed very little over the years" (Cummins, 1996, p 34). That survey shows that 13% of Income Support claimants had contacted the DSS/ BA helpline for information; 5% acquired their information from a DSS/BA leaflet; and 3% from a poster – none had acted on information from a DSS advertisement on television or in the press. It also shows that 27% regarded information about income support as 'common knowledge', and 14% had learned about it from friends or relatives (Cummins, 1996).

Another study of first-time claimants of income support (Williams et al, 1995) finds that 49% regarded it as common knowledge or 'just knew' about it, while 2% had information from television, radio or a magazine. In this study, no claimants received information from friends, relations or from a leaflet, many of which are reported to be ignored or discarded. Research for the DSS, which aimed to "improve and understand the ways in which customers receive and utilise information", finds that:

> A few people had picked up leaflets while waiting at the benefit office for
> an interview.... The evidence suggests that many Income Support claimants
> are not really 'readers' by habit or ability. (Bailey and Pyres, 1996, p 1)

Stafford et al (1996, p 13) agree that "Leaflets do not appear to be a particularly salient feature in raising general awareness, or in the decision of first time applicants to obtain an application form". These findings are confirmed by Cummins and Spilsbury (1998, p 20), who, in a survey of people who had recently enquired about a benefit, conclude: "Overall the popularity of some kind of personal contact is important". A senior official put it this way:

> "One of the things about benefits is that they are more personal, more
> word-of-mouth perhaps. Maybe you could be persuaded about a Mars Bar
> without being told by your old auntie that they are nice, whereas with
> benefits you tend to visit your old auntie rather than advertising. Word-of-
> mouth is much more important. Any research we did always demonstrated
> that people had heard from somebody else."

These findings are important: not only do they highlight the difficulty of informing people, but they also demonstrate that to carry on disseminating information in the same old ways is unlikely to be effective. The continuing reliance on leaflets, for example, needs to be reassessed. A more radical or different approach is needed if the aim of information policy is to increase the awareness of eligible people about their rights.

There is another important point about the nature of information and of claimants' perceptions of different sources of information. Here, again, there is no lack of evidence:

> Information and advice are not neutral, but are judged and evaluated in the light of their source.... The sources ... are judged in terms of whose side they are perceived to be on. (Vincent et al, 1995, p 73)

> The lack of trust in the Benefits Agency still seems relatively common. It may inhibit effective communication. (Stafford et al, 1996, p 16)

One local authority welfare rights worker was more forthright: "I'm not even sure that at the moment the DSS are the best people to promote benefits. They have not got the credibility, that's the trouble".

Paradoxically, there is also evidence to show that while informal sources are more commonly used, people getting information primarily from formal sources were more likely to make use of the services. Those who are eligible but do not use services were more likely to have heard of them through informal sources (Silverstein, 1984). This complicates the picture for providers of information, already faced with a difficult task, and underlines the importance of effective government information.

Sources of information are not exclusive, however (Vincent et al, 1995; Stafford et al, 1996). Potential claimants may check the information given to them, for example by the Job Centre, with their local Citizens' Advice Bureau, and vice versa, or information from a website with their councillor. Each source may have either credibility problems or perceived advantages for potential claimants. An apparent wealth of sources of information would seem to be at odds with the acknowledged low levels of take-up of some benefits.

This section has provided some explanations and shown that for potential claimants the picture is complex. It puts the strategic importance of government provision into context. Although claimants have no choice about benefits themselves or where to go to make a claim, they can decide where to go for information about their entitlements. As discussed earlier, this book does not ignore the existence of the many other valuable sources of information for potential claimants. Nor does it deny the important role of the many agencies whose raison d'être is to enable people to claim their entitlements. Although questions are raised by this study about the role of such agencies in filling the information gaps left by central and local government, this is not the place to address their contribution to informing the public. The focus here is on government information policy and what can be learnt from that about attitudes towards – and definitions of – citizenship.

Information: claiming behaviour

An understanding of claiming behaviour is also important for information policy makers. Corden (1995), for example, observes that research in the 1980s that helped to understand claiming behaviour has in turn helped to improve government information strategies and increase take-up rates for some social security benefits. Models of claiming behaviour show information to be one important factor in the claiming process. The process does not always follow an apparently rational sequence (Deacon and Bradshaw, 1983; Craig, 1991; Corden, 1999). Information needs are personal and complex: "People do not always perceive that they have a need for information" (Hughes and Moore, 1993, p 32); "Stigma ... could inhibit the absorption of information about benefits" (Craig, 1991, p 543). There may be more fundamental deprivational barriers, such as poor levels of literacy or sociological or psychological reasons for an individual's unwillingness to seek or act on information. Even 'good' information does not necessarily result in a claim from those who are eligible. Models of claiming behaviour can provide a way of understanding.

The Kerr 'threshold model' (Kerr, 1982) of the claiming process regards information as just one threshold in a set sequence which together result in a claim being made. The six necessary conditions, or 'constructs', for claiming are:

- perceived need;
- basic knowledge;
- perceived eligibility;
- perceived utility;
- beliefs and feelings;
- perceived stability of circumstances.

Kerr developed the model to investigate differential take-up rates of Supplementary Pension. It has been very influential on the development of further models which have attempted to overcome some of its shortcomings (Buckland and Dawson, 1989; Craig, 1991; van Oorschot, 1991; Corden, 1999).

Ritchie and Matthew's 'trade-off' model emphasises the critical role of perceptions of need and eligibility, located in "a tightly knit cluster of ethical, factual and emotional notions about who could and should receive the benefit" (in Craig, 1991, p 548). Perceptions of eligibility require information about benefits and a strong perception of need makes absorbing information easier. This model suggests that very low levels of basic knowledge do not necessarily prevent claiming. The role of other people in encouraging claims is recognised when would-be claimants weigh up the pros and cons of claiming (Craig, 1991; Corden, 1999). Graham (in Craig, 1991) regarded basic knowledge as critical: both the source and the content of information are important. The effort people make for themselves to seek information and assess their own eligibility is the major distinguishing factor between claimants and non-claimants.

This balance between 'active' governments and 'active' citizens is also important to van Oorschot's 'three-t-model'. This model, based on international comparisons, concludes that take-up is the result of the interaction of three levels:

- the benefit scheme itself;
- the administrative level (which includes information provision);
- the client level (which includes insufficient knowledge or ignorance).

Importantly for this study, the model shows that it is not enough to understand claimants' own behaviour to account for low levels of take-up; rather, "Policy-makers and administrators can often be held responsible too" (van Oorschot, 1991, p 20).

An understanding of claiming behaviour intensifies the need for information providers to assess their purpose, as well as the methods they use. It tests their commitment to enabling citizens to claim their entitlements. It is generally accepted that the better off are better informed about benefits and "find claiming less uncertain and less troublesome" (Craig, 1991, p 554), and that "Minority groups are often excluded from mainstream sources of information and advice, which may not in any case meet their needs" (Steele, 1997, p 300). Key findings from research also indicate that publicity needs to concentrate on sharpening the perceptions of eligibility rather than just increasing general awareness of the existence of benefits (Craig, 1991). However, "Perceptions of eligibility are formed from a complex of relevant and irrelevant attitudes and beliefs" (Craig, 1991, p 557). Having been refused once, many claimants are likely to be deterred from making further claims in the future when they may in fact be eligible (Cohen and Tarpey, 1986; Craig, 1991; Corden, 1995).

There are many factors that encourage or prevent claimants receiving their entitlements. This book focuses on one factor: government information policy. A willingness by governments to assist claimants to overcome some of the barriers, or a decision to erect or ignore barriers, will not only influences claimants' ability to receive entitlements but also indicate government attitudes to citizenship rights.

FOUR

Social democracy and information

The postwar welfare state was built around the idea of citizenship as an inclusive concept compensating for the inequalities of class and of the market. This social democratic consensus required a strong bureaucratic state as provider of services designed to improve conditions in a capitalist society. Social democrats believe in a reformist welfare state, a state "capable of enhancing the welfare of all" (Kearns, 1997, p 12). The concept of citizenship defined the relationship between individuals and the state and mediated entitlements to state organised welfare:

> The new services ... treat the individual as a citizen, not as a 'pauper', an object of charity or a member of a particular social class. (*The Times*, 1948)

It was assumed that the state, or experts, knew best (Alcock, 1989; Sullivan, 1998). They were possessors of information, in an unequal relationship in which potential users were regarded as passive recipients. The corollary is a state that accepts responsibility to inform, and sets up the administration to do so. Effective information about all benefits to all citizens would need to be an integral part of the new welfare state. Writing about the postwar services, Marshall (1967, p 118) was convinced that government had to be proactive:

> The new welfare services must decide how far they should go in publicising their wares, and we may note that the giving of information about the available services was the first of the activities assigned by the National Assistance Act to the Local Welfare Authority.

National Assistance, 1948-66

The new benefits that resulted from the 1946 National Insurance Act and the 1948 National Assistance Act followed the recommendations of the 1942 Beveridge Report, 'Social Insurance and Allied Services'. They formed part of wider radical social policy reforms that together became known as the 'welfare state'. The report led to a new system of financial assistance for those without other adequate income. It caught the imagination of a large majority of the population of wartime Britain, a time during which previously unknown levels of poverty had been revealed. There was anticipation of a better future, and therefore popular support for, and sympathy with, proposals for social reform (Fraser, 1984; Lowe, 1990).

The ground had been well prepared for government dissemination of information about the new services and benefits by Beveridge himself. His determination to gain government acceptance for his proposals (see Golding and Middleton, 1982; Leaper, 1991; Sullivan, 1996), and forestall cabinet sceptics, was arguably rather more important to him than the information needs of citizens exercising their rights. At the time, the Treasury was sceptical of the proposed reforms and was never "instinctively pro-welfare" (Deakin and Parry, 2000, p 21). Barnett (1987, p 27) describes "Beveridge who in masterly style leaked news of the sweeter chocolates in his welfare assortment to the press, in order to whet public appetite and so bring pressure on the Cabinet". This wide coverage helped, inter alia, to disseminate information to the public about the popular proposals for a 'welfare state' (Golding and Middleton, 1982; Leaper, 1991).

However, Beveridge was also aware that a new and inevitably complex system could cause difficulties for people wanting to claim their entitlements, even when the system was unified and simplified in the way he proposed. He suggested ways to inform the public that clearly placed the responsibility on government:

> The social security system … must still be a machine with many parts and complications to deal with all the complexities of need and variety of persons. Citizens cannot be left to find out all about it by reading official pamphlets, however clearly they may be written. There should be in every local [social] Security Office an Advice Bureau to which every person in doubt or difficulty can be referred and which will be able to tell him, not only about the official provision for social security but about all the other organs – official, semi-official and voluntary, central or local – which may be able to help him in his difficulty. (Beveridge, 1942, p 148)

His recommendation was not followed. The 1948 Act places no more than an implicit and unspecified duty to inform on the officers of the National Assistance Board (NAB), who were "to exercise their functions in such a manner as shall best promote the welfare of the persons affected" (section 2.1).

The postwar Labour government attempted to influence public attitudes with widespread publicity about welfare services. According to Lowe (1990), they did so hoping thereby to assure the longer-term success of the welfare state. It was clearly important to the government's credibility that the new services should succeed. Lowe, however, detects widespread public ignorance about welfare policy across the board from the start. This was due to the government's 'ineffectual' information policies, technical inadequacies and, most importantly,

> the Cabinet, which not only lacked the political will to develop a coherent strategy but also equated the inspirational messages, by which significant changes in public attitude could alone be affected, with party politics and

consequently adjudged them to be an inappropriate use of tax-payers' money. (Lowe, 1990, p 180)

The overwhelming government rhetoric, however, was one of informing and encouraging potential claimants, and there is evidence of planned information policy to enable 'social citizens' to claim their rights. Much of the initiative and drive came from the Minister for National Insurance, James Griffiths, who was "determined to break from the atmosphere of the Poor Law" (Timmins, 1995, p 138). The rhetoric was matched by action. Leaflets, posters and booklets to inform the public and advisers were from the start the main method of disseminating information about the social security system. Fifty million leaflets were printed in 1948 to provide information on benefits and contributions. They were too often "dense, difficult to read and very 'official'" (DSS, 1998b, p 1), drably produced on flimsy and rather grey postwar paper which, perhaps only in retrospect, look neither attractive nor encouraging to potential claimants. The comprehensive 1948 'Family Guide to the National Insurance Scheme', which included information about National Assistance (NA), is a pocket-sized booklet which cost the public one penny to buy. The Foreword, signed by Griffiths, is paternalistic – "I am afraid you will find some parts complicated" – and in tune with the times, but it also uses language which is enthusiastic about the new services and clearly worded to encourage claims.

However, within a policy of encouraging claims there soon emerged a tension in the difficult balance between the competing demands of rising public expenditure and improving the public's awareness of rights to benefits. One small but interesting example illustrates the point. An unsigned NAB memo, likely to be from the early 1950s, suggests that leaflets NI 49 and NI 49A (concerned with grants for deaths abroad) be combined to remove duplication of information. The explicit aim was to save £16 per year. The memo adds that "more important than this small saving, however, is the removal of inconvenience to the reader and the staff time involved in ordering and controlling stocks of the smaller of the leaflets" (NAB, nd). The suggestion was taken up, satisfying all those concerned about better information, the scheme's administrators, and those who held the purse strings.

The climate of encouragement to claim was officially demonstrated in the Report of the National Assistance Board for the year ended 31 December 1949, which for the first time includes a section entitled 'Publicity'. It accepts the responsibility for active provision of information and acknowledges that "changes in administrative arrangements do not quickly become part of general knowledge" (NAB, 1949, p 18). It also acknowledges the difficulties for the NAB in providing brief and accurate information about a complex system of benefits without misleading and raising the hopes of those not eligible. These difficulties might be expected to deter information providers.

Another positive picture of that time is that of NAB officers carrying the book of rules around in their pocket, rules that were understood and applied (Donnison, 1982). The officers were keen to assist and encourage applications from those who were entitled. If this is indeed a true picture, it provides evidence of an attitude among civil servants at the sharp end, of 'street level bureaucrats' (Lipsky, 1980), whose role in making policy must not be ignored. Fine words from the top are of no help to potential claimants should officials in contact with the public be unable or unwilling, for whatever reason, to act in accordance with them.

However, part of the explanation for this commitment to inform, at both central policy maker and local officer level, was the drive to ensure the success of the new schemes. In the words of one politician:

> "That must almost by definition, I would have thought, have been true in the immediate aftermath of 1948, because apart from anything else you have a completely new system which depended on people transferring into it, or getting into it, from a whole variety of bits and pieces of schemes that had existed before."

The success of the welfare state in eradicating poverty was proclaimed by both government and opposition in the 1950s (Curran, 1960; Crosland, 1964). In a climate of optimism, it suited both political parties to believe that the new welfare state was working. Were that the case, it could arguably lessen the need for active promotion of social security benefits and a more complacent attitude towards providing information at that time would not be surprising.

The annual reports of the NAB published during the 1950s do not contain a section on publicity. The reports simply refer in the text to the NAB's reliance on people calling into the office, requesting a home visit or sending in a claim form obtained from a post office. Webb's (1975, p 467) description of "the quiet obscurity into which the administration of national assistance had sunk in the mid-fifties" could be based on the belief that people were receiving their entitlements, rather than an unwillingness to promote benefits.

An alternative explanation for the 'low-key' approach to information could be that it was the beginning of a response to worries about the financial and moral need to deter claims. If so, this would have implications for information policy and for universal social rights, reflecting shifting attitudes to citizenship. At this time, there is certainly criticism of financial extravagance in meeting the needs of the poor (Hill, 1993; Alcock, 1999). There is also evidence that the attitudes and values of government and other institutions influenced information policy.

The plight of lone mothers demonstrates a deliberate policy to withhold information from one group of recipients. Many 'natural mothers' from the 1940s, 1950s and 1960s say they were never informed that they were eligible for National Assistance (NPSG, personal communication, 1999). The result was that babies were reluctantly given up for adoption because those mothers were told they had no other option. Marsden (1969, p 242) finds evidence of:

an unexpressed conspiracy of silence – most importantly between the NAB and the influential problem-page writers of the women's magazines – which effectively conceals the availability of support for the woman who wishes to live apart from her husband and for the unmarried mother who wants to bring up her child alone. The National Assistance Regulations, or the officers' application of them ... have the appearance of seeking to defend marriage. (Marsden, 1969, p 242)

Further evidence from Natural Parents Support Group (NPSG) finds that social workers at that time also withheld information. Their justification for doing so was to avoid the inevitable stigma for unmarried mothers by reflecting the morals of wider society. However, there is also evidence that mother and baby homes had a financial incentive to get as many women as possible to give up their babies, because they could expect a donation from the satisfied adoptive couple (BBC, 1999; NPSG, personal communication, 1999).

The UK was not alone in finding that the moral climate at that time made it politically difficult to mount any sort of campaign to increase awareness of rights to benefit among unmarried mothers and pregnant women. A survey in New York in 1965 found that many endured poverty because they were ignorant of what they could claim.

> Welfare departments never conduct public information campaigns about the availability of legal benefits, for if people are ignorant of entitlements, many will not apply, and many of those who do can be arbitrarily brushed aside as ineligible. (Piven and Cloward, 1972, p 150)

This group of women was unlikely to make a fuss, or to query information and advice by seeking publicity, despite the implications for both themselves and their babies. This 'political' argument for information policy also reflects the overt power of those who have information and the lack of citizenship status of this group of women.

Doubts were also beginning to be expressed in the 1950s concerning the success of the new social security scheme in eradicating poverty. The 'rediscovery of poverty' was based on government studies and on academic research in the 1950s and 1960s (Phillips Committee, 1954; Townsend, 1963; Abel-Smith and Townsend, 1965; MPNI, 1966; Atkinson, 1969; Bull, 1971). The research shows that people were losing – or not receiving – benefit because they did not know their rights, and that low take-up was in part at least a result of ignorance. Criticism of the ineffectiveness of the NAB in informing people of their eligibility – for whatever reason – raised questions about where the responsibility should lie. Writing in 1958, Abel-Smith (1958, p 71), for example, asks:

> how is the citizen going to know what services are available and how to use them?... It is not enough to stick up closely printed notices outside the post

office.... What we need is a citizens' office in every town run on public money ... independent ... specially trained staff not enthusiastic amateurs.

In the first half of the 1960s, an information unit was set up within the NAB, confirming a shift in attitude towards a more proactive policy. Its annual reports begin again to explicitly recognise the importance and the difficulties of information giving and the rights of claimants:

> The Board's special problem has always been to ensure that those who are in need have readily available to them, at the time they require it, the information which will tell them about the help which they can get and how to set about getting a continuing and effective information service for the public and the Press. (NAB, 1960, p 41)

The 1965 version of 'Everybody's Guide to National Insurance', now costing 10 pence, explains that "National Assistance ... is available as a right for people with insufficient resources.... It is important for all of us to understand our rights and our obligations" (MPNI, 1965, p 1). The rhetoric of official reports in the early 1960s is again matched by national and local publicity in an effort to inform and encourage claimants. Posters and leaflets were supplemented by 'invitations to claim' placed in retirement pension books. The NAB's area managers were required to give information and publicity a priority on both their time and their resources.

The evidence is contradictory about whether these positive attitudes and words resulted in effective information policy to enable people to claim their benefit entitlements. According to Deacon and Bradshaw (1983, p 104) there was an improvement, even if not a wholehearted one:

> In the early 1960s the Board began to improve its publicity material, and extend and refashion the training it provided for its staff. This however, was opposed by some of its senior officials who were still committed to the procedures and practices which they believed to have been so successful in the earlier years.

Deacon and Bradshaw also recognise that there remained a legacy of stigma for NA claimants, despite the efforts of the late 1940s. Webb (1975) agrees that there was a contrast with the service provided for claimants of National Insurance benefits, citing different styles and approaches in the leaflets. Information policy was reflecting different attitudes to different claimant groups and to their status as citizens with rights to claim.

Others see little evidence of the social democratic ideal and do not agree with Deacon and Bradshaw's guarded support for the NAB's policy. Looking back over this period, Hill (1976, p 65) comments on government attitudes and practice:

There has been no lack of evidence in recent years of absence of adequate information about benefits. The most extreme cases of this involve an almost total failure to provide information even on request. It is hard to see how this sort of behaviour can be explained except in terms of a wilful desire to restrict demand.

Glennerster (1962, p 11), supporting the need for more proactive and effective information, detects tensions and ambivalence as explanations for limited activity:

At present the Board [NAB] seems afraid to publicise its services widely. On the other hand, it also seems to feel that perhaps it ought to do *some* publicity. It ends up pottering around with posters and playing at public relations.... It seems afraid to raise its voice too much in case too many people hear. (emphasis in original)

Supplementary Benefits, 1966-88

Changes to the social security system following the 1966 Ministry of Social Security Act were in part intended to increase take-up of benefits and to overcome some of the difficulties associated with NA (Atkinson, 1969; Foster, 1983). Attracting more claimants "would depend on the success of the publicity given to the new benefits" (Webb, 1975, p 458). Ignorance and low take-up were a concern of academics and burgeoning pressure groups (Atkinson, 1969; Deacon and Bradshaw, 1983). Benefit levels increased and there was an expressed 'right' to benefit for those who met the qualifying conditions (Foster, 1983; Hill, 1990; Alcock, 1999). It was anticipated that an additional 250,000 people would claim, at a cost of £13 million. Perhaps this is further evidence of a shift back to a policy of encouraging citizens to exercise their rights. There had already been a 25.1% increase in social security spending between 1960 and 1964 (Golding and Middleton, 1982, p 226).

The Supplementary Benefits Commission (SBC) was set up to administer the new scheme as part of the new Ministry of Social Security (MSS), merging the NAB and the Ministry of Pensions and National Assistance (MPNI). This reorganisation was in part an attempt to reduce the deterrent effect of the legacy of the Poor Law, including the stigma of means testing (Atkinson, 1969; Deacon and Bradshaw, 1983; Foster, 1983). There was to be an "emphasis placed by the Commission on advertising and publicity" (Briggs and Rees, 1980, p 4), but again no positive duty placed on officials to seek out and inform eligible non-claimants. A proposal to do so had been rejected (Webb, 1975).

In response to changing attitudes, the second half of the 1960s saw a lot of publicity activity: "During the 1960s, in the era of welfare expansion … programmes are published" (Cox, 1998, p 7). The rhetoric of rights was translated into official acknowledgement that lack of information results in low take-up:

after the passing of the Ministry of Social Security Act, 1966, a sea-change came over the Commission's attitude to advertising its wares: in particular … the concept of 'entitlement' had been accorded greater and greater prominence. (Briggs and Rees, 1980, p 146)

In the 1967 edition of 'Everybody's Guide to Social Security', which cost the public one shilling to buy, the Minister of Social Security, Judith Hart, wrote:

It is most important that we should all know our rights, and that we should know the rules of the system…. And I should like to emphasise to you that supplementary benefits are a right. Please claim them.

The rhetoric is supported by other evidence of the Labour government's positive attitude to providing information about benefits. The Working Party on Public Awareness of Social Service Benefits (including Supplementary Benefit) was set up in July 1968. It decided to meet on a confidential basis in order to avoid giving the impression that comprehensive changes were necessarily being prepared. In a note to the Working Party, dated 15 May 1968 (but not open for public inspection until 1999), the author CSA wrote:

Fundamentally, she [the Minister] is concerned to secure greater awareness on the part of the consumers of the benefits provided under our schemes, and greater understanding of the reasons why the schemes do what they do and not do what they don't do. (MSS, 1968a)

Also, in 1968 the MSS published 'The Consumer Side of Benefits', which was a "summary of work done and methods employed by the MSS to keep the public informed of their entitlement to benefit under the various schemes" (MSS, 1968b, p 1). It reported that, in 1967, 56 million leaflets were printed and special campaigns mounted when big changes were introduced. There was also almost daily contact with television, radio and the press. Local office managers were again encouraged "to secure a better local understanding of Social Security matters" (MSS, 1968b, p 21). The document concluded that people in the main knew about National Insurance Benefits and Family Allowances and had an increasing awareness about Supplementary Benefits (MSS, 1968b).

Despite the government's renewed efforts to inform people of their rights, not everyone agreed that they were doing enough. There was criticism that what they were doing was ineffective (Golding and Middleton, 1982). Their motives were questioned, and there was suspicion that the information agenda was not straightforwardly an attempt to enable people to exercise their rights. What is the evidence to support these claims?

The Child Poverty Action Group (CPAG) had been founded in 1965 as a campaigning organisation to press for adequate levels of income for those on benefit. It detects other reasons for decisions about information provision:

> We pass legislation to provide a variety of doles for which those who need them can apply…. Yet we refuse to tell people clearly and simply what help is available to them, lest they should come to regard it as a right…. We have drawn attention to the failure of both central government and local authorities to provide adequate information about people's rights … there are those who believe that telling people of their rights would open the floodgates of abuse. (CPAG, 1967, p 2)

The brief history of the proposed 'Short Step' campaign illustrates some of the arguments. The minister, Judith Hart, planned an 'entitlement campaign' to begin in June 1968. With Treasury approval, over 14 million leaflets entitled 'The Short Step' were to be distributed, explaining the various means-tested benefits that were available for low-income families. The leaflet – DW 9309 (see Appendix B) – was well produced, clearly set out and encouraging in its tone: "Remember: this is not charity but your right". This shift in attitude was applauded by CPAG:

> The emphasis throughout the campaign will be that all the benefits which exist, from welfare foods to rate rebates, are a right. (CPAG, 1968a, p 7)

Hart asked for the support of MPs in disseminating information about the benefits (*Hansard*, 15 July 1968, col 1017). However, after a promising start, the campaign was delayed. Other agendas were suspected:

> Can it be that somebody in the Treasury had woken up to the financial implications of encouraging people to claim all their rights?… One begins to suspect that there is something inherent in benefits designed for the poor which makes for poor publicity and poor administration. (CPAG, 1968b, p 3)

The suspicions of CPAG seemed to be well founded. They are corroborated in the diaries of the Secretary of State for Social Services at that time, Richard Crossman, who expresses his ambivalence towards publicity and his "publicity problem with Judith Hart" (Crossman, 1977, p 134). He records that normally he would have been very keen to promote benefits, but increasing public concern about benefit scroungers led him skilfully to 'divert' the Minister:

> What's certain is how obviously unaware she is of the danger that a too well-advertised entitlement campaign may actually excite public agitation against scrounging … where publicity is concerned we're a lamentably deficient government. (Crossman, 1977, p 135)

The national campaign was postponed in favour of a pilot scheme in selected areas. That scheme failed to provide the hoped-for means of assessing the effectiveness of different methods of distribution. The campaign was dropped. Bull (1970) sees this as a 'sad symbol' of the waning of the government's earlier enthusiasm for informing claimants of their rights. He suspects 'Treasury meanness' or worries about administrative overload:

> One realises how any attempt to launch an official campaign is at the mercy of politicians and officials who may wish to suppress information about rights. (Bull, 1970, p 9)

CPAG was also critical of the failure of the scheme but acknowledged a change in attitude demonstrated by the Minister, even though she was overruled:

> This is a disgraceful story of official evasion, prevarication and incompetence ... nothing to do with research.... The more likely explanation is either Treasury meanness or interdepartmental wrangling.... It is only fair to say that the campaign was devised with the best of intentions by a Minister (Judith Hart) who was genuinely concerned about the failure of so many means-tested benefits to reach the families of low-paid workers ... but good intentions are not enough if such exercises are to produce results. (CPAG, 1969, p 16)

After early promises and initiatives following the legislation of 1966, the aborted campaign provides more evidence of a shift in information policy, and of the gap between the rhetoric and the reality. Policy had moved away from the initial enthusiasm and planned campaigns to encourage all citizens to claim their rights and was determined by concerns about resources and abuse of the system.

However, this shift failed to hide the extent of ignorance of claimants. In his introduction to the 1970 Supplementary Benefits Commission Handbook, the Chairman, Lord Collison, acknowledged:

> The Commission recognise that some people when supplementary benefits could be of real help to them do not claim and that lack of awareness of what they might receive by way of support from the scheme is a factor in failure to claim. (SBC/DHSS, 1970, p 2)

The intentions of information policy makers, however, continued to be unclear. Briggs and Rees (1980) for example, observe that government departments from the mid-1960s were increasingly willing to devote effort and resources to providing information. Others are more critical:

> The first and most critical requirement for good take-up is that those eligible must know of the existence of the benefit.... The Department of Health and Social Security and the Department of the Environment have both made various efforts to publicise certain benefits, but, considering the expenditure involved, the results have not been spectacular. Approaches

> have been at best pedestrian.... They rarely try to 'sell' their product. (Simkins and Tickner, 1978, p 171)

Under a Conservative government, the Department of the Environment mounted what was at that time the most expensive campaign ever. It spent £997,400 between September 1972 and February 1974 to promote rent rebates and allowances (Deacon and Bradshaw, 1983), despite this being one of the few benefits for which there was a statutory duty placed on local authorities to inform all tenants (see Appendix A of this book to put these figures into context). The strategic importance of the campaign can be explained in part by the removal of central government subsidies under the 1972 Housing Finance Act. Publicity about help with housing costs could reduce the politically damaging effect of increased rents and limit conflict between central government and local authorities. The campaign was also part of the wider debate about the future of social security; that is, whether it should be based on principles of universality or selectivity.

There is also evidence of other agendas. The 1967 edition of the CPAG Handbook, an annual publication designed to give potential claimants and others information about entitlement to all benefits, was labelled a 'scrounger's charter' by Conservative MPs and some of the press (Golding and Middleton, 1982, p 100). In 1973 a report on exceptional needs payments concluded that the SBC:

> fear that an 'advertising campaign' would do more harm than good by stimulating a flood of unsuccessful claims.... They [claimants] should not, says this policy, be misled by rash promises to become discontented with things as they are. Such poverty, after all, is not really exceptional, but more or less in the everyday run of things. (Cited in Jordan, 1974, p 69)

Jordan (1974) comments on the effectiveness of the rationing of Supplementary Benefit exceptional needs payments by ignorance, and by the 'bogey of abuse'. Parker (1975, p 152) suspects that information policy that leaves the initiative with the claimant is "a device to limit claims on public funds". Briggs and Rees' earlier optimism at the introduction of Supplementary Benefit, with its emphasis on rights and information, turns out to have been misplaced at a time of economic recession.

> At a time of retrenchment one can hardly feel optimistic about any proposal that would increase public expenditure through the equitable increase in take-up of benefits. Public ignorance and apathy have their attractions for any government obsessed with the Public Sector Borrowing Requirement. (Briggs and Rees, 1980, p 154)

Simkins and Tickner (1978, p 170), writing about benefits for disabled people, agree:

> For some benefits much effort has been invested in attempts to improve take-up. On the other hand, it has on occasion seemed to be a deliberate policy to avoid efforts to achieve good take-up in order to avoid the consequent cost and associated budgetary embarrassment.

Deakin and Parry (2000) comment that wider economic difficulties in this period obscured the original rationale of benefits.

Some observers suspect that complex schemes have their own attraction for information policy makers. Hill (1976, p 64) for example, writes:

> Radical critics of the social security system argue that the obscurity of some of the benefit provisions and the absence of publicity about rights can be directly explained by a desire to reduce demand for benefits.

Writing about the 1978 review of the scheme, Donnison (1982, p 144) agrees:

> Most people, it soon became clear, found the whole scheme bewildering, and many were convinced that it had been made deliberately incomprehensible to prevent people from claiming benefits.

Nevertheless, the information machine continued to roll on. The mainstay of the Department of Health and Social Security's (DHSS) efforts during the 1970s continued to be leaflets and posters. The 1978 version of 'Which Benefit?' (FB20), a well designed, encouraging and clearly set out leaflet, gave brief details of all social security benefits. It begins with these words:

> Knowing which ones you're entitled to, and how to claim them, can be a problem. This booklet tells you which and how…. Even if you can't claim anything now, keep this booklet handy. There may be a day when you – or someone you know – will need it.

In the House of Commons, Mr Brotherton asked the Secretary of State for Social Services how many copies of the booklet had been printed and distributed, and the total cost to public funds. The Minister, Mr Orme, replied:

> 400,000 copies of the new booklet 'Which Benefit' have been printed so far…. Total cost was £26,000…. Since 1970 the Department's policy has been to make booklets of this kind available free of charge so as to get the widest possible distribution among those who are eligible for the benefits but may not have sufficient money to pay for booklets. (*Hansard*, 5 December 1978, col 620)

Perhaps, in the light of much of the above evidence, this shows an unexpected commitment to helping people to exercise their rights and illustrates the often paradoxical nature of information policy.

Summary

During this period of social democracy, there had clearly been a general shift away from a comprehensive and planned information policy intended to reach all potential claimants. There is evidence of concern about claimants' ignorance of their entitlements, of good initiatives, and of comprehensive and effective information. However, there is also evidence of information policy based on considerations of financial resources, and on fears about raising expectations, abuse and encouraging scroungers. Policy was sensitive also to public opinion and reflected the moral values and attitudes of politicians and others. No longer were benefits promoted unquestionably as an inherent part of citizenship for all those who were eligible.

FIVE

The New Right and information

The Conservative Party formed the government in 1979, and was led by Margaret Thatcher. These words epitomised her neoliberal philosophy:

> There is no such thing as society…. There are individual men and women, and there are families…. It's our duty to look after ourselves. (Thatcher, quoted in Lund, 1999, p 449)

Her political agenda was driven by the aims of 'rolling back the state' and of reinstating market values, family values and individual choice (Williams, 1999). Although in many ways the welfare state would stay substantially intact (King and Waldron, 1988; Cochrane and Clarke, 1993), there is a general view that her administration completed the gradual fracturing of the postwar welfare consensus (Sullivan, 1996). In doing so, it aimed to change the nature of the relationship between the state and individuals by reinforcing individual responsibility and reducing dependency.

There were clear signs of change that would impact on information policy. The intention of the government seemed to be to develop a more residual welfare state (Hewitt, 1999). Growing welfare expenditure was perceived as retarding economic growth (Heywood, 1992). The recession of the 1970s had resulted in more people being eligible for benefits, while at the same time governments felt the need to pursue austerity measures in public spending. In an unfavourable economic climate, there was hostility to the social security system and to claimants (Walker, 1982). A welfare state originally aiming to alleviate poverty and provide the security of a basic income for all was criticised for encouraging dependency (Cox, 1998).

Definitions of citizenship and the balance between rights and responsibilities explicitly shifted. Lister (1998b, p 312) observes that, after 1979, there was:

> A concerted ideological attack on the post-war social democratic conception of citizenship. Notions of community and collective welfare were cast aside before the altar of individualism, enterprise and consumerism.

The implication of the New Right philosophy for the provision of information about welfare entitlements is complex and sometimes contradictory. Market liberals whose overriding concern is with choice and consumerism would be expected to be generally in favour of disseminating information to enable people to make choices. Thatcher's government was anxious to change what were seen as ingrained attitudes to the welfare state. This pedagogic mission could be seen to add pressure to provide more – not less – information. For others, however, information about entitlements might be considered a temptation to 'scrounge' (Jacobs, 1994), where "'welfare' came to imply not support for those in need but a subsidy to dependency" (Deakin and Parry, 2000, p 114). The message was clear: "low take-up is seen to reflect a (laudable) reluctance on the part of the citizen to rely on state benefits" (Cook, 1989, p 123). These latter concerns would be likely to persuade the government that information provision about welfare services and benefits should be less than universal.

However, two examples show no such reluctance to inform. First, the government's campaign to encourage people to enrol in private pension schemes. This was based on the need to reduce public expenditure and on a belief in the values of individual responsibility. For Walker (1999, p 513), both issues "were underpinned by the same neoliberal ideology". Attractive state-funded incentives were heavily publicised in an effective campaign which resulted in five million people contributing by 1993, "far surpassing the half million employees expected by the government" (Ginn and Arber, 2000, p 208). Departmental reports do not detail the expenditure on the campaign, although it was clearly not constrained by resources. One politician remembered it this way:

> "They [the Tories] went in the 1986 Act into private pensions in a big way. They went for a 2% bribe which was advertised and advertised ... that was the only occasion when I think the Tories put an effort into promoting policy. You find it happens when there's a sea-change in the social security system."

It was later estimated that three million people were sold private pensions when they would have been better off staying in the state scheme (Walker, 1999).

The second example concerns the 1980 Housing Act, which placed a duty on landlords to inform tenants of their 'Right to Buy' their home. During the 1980s, £2.3 million was spent on promoting council house sales (see Appendix A of this book to put this figure into context). The campaign can be understood by the political importance of the 'Right to Buy' legislation. It was an electoral asset (Malpass and Murie, 1994). It was also consistent with the government's ideal of a property owning democracy (Forrest and Murie, 1991), defining what it is to be a citizen in a market-oriented society. The campaign was about rights based on financial ability and on eligibility to become self-reliant owner-occupiers, rather than to remain as dependent tenants. Those unable to exercise this right too often became marginalised. Forrest and Murie (1991, p 207) express the strategic importance of ongoing information and publicity about the scheme thus:

> The political and financial importance of this legislation meant that the task was not completed with the passage of legislation.

Were these 'political' campaigns exceptional or part of a planned shift in information policy? By the 1980s there was a determination to cut back increases in public expenditure (Burchardt and Hills, 1999). Social security was not a priority for Thatcher (Alcock, 1990); instead, it became "an ideologically contested area…. The Treasury … [was] driven by the belief that there were substantial economies to be made" (Deakin and Parry, 2000, p 112). Together, these factors easily translate into a less active government, providing less information about services and benefits, and interfering less in the lives of its citizens. The corollary is that people would need to be more active in finding out for themselves and, presumably, responsible for the consequences of their own ignorance. One senior official remembered the change:

> "I was at the DHSS for a short time before the change of government. There was a very large shift then. One of the things just after the government came in in 1979, that was a major shift – things were different then – people expected to find out for themselves. The ethos continued in many ways … policy staff were not enthusiastic about communicating with people."

The 1980 Social Security Act made important changes to the supplementary benefits scheme. It aimed yet again for simplification, for a clearer understanding for both staff and claimants (Walker, 1982), and for greater publicity for the system (Birch, 1983). The Supplementary Benefits Commission (SBC) was abolished. However, the scheme remained complex. It was not easier for claimants to know their rights (Foster, 1983). The legislation itself limited the duty on officers to "exercise their functions in such a manner as shall best promote the welfare of persons affected by the exercise of those functions" (1980 Social Security Act, para 27.[i]).

In the early 1980s, however, departmental reports continued to acknowledge that a 'significant proportion' of those entitled to some means-tested benefits were not claiming them:

> Lack of knowledge could be a reason, although substantial efforts are made to inform potential claimants of their entitlement to benefit. (DHSS, 1983, p 63)

> The best service the DHSS can give to recipients and potential recipients is to … make sure that people know about and receive their legal entitlement … efforts are being made to improve advice and information about the benefits available. (DHSS, 1985, p 177)

Although the evidence shows a shift to targeting information, there were some publicity innovations in the early 1980s to inform *all* potential claimants. One notable and successful innovation was the introduction, in 1984, of the telephone information line, 'Freeline'. This averaged 20,000 calls per month in its first six months from people wanting general information about benefits. By April

1986, the monthly figure had risen to 50,000 (this service is described in more detail later in this chapter).

In another paradoxical move, the design of leaflets improved and some were introduced in ethnic minority languages. The style and language of leaflets generally became more encouraging to potential claimants. For example, the 1982 leaflet for supplementary benefit (SB 21) asks, "Need more money? Here's how to claim". It is bright and well designed, and has a 'user friendly' explanation of what the benefits are, who qualifies, and a pictorial sequence of events for claiming it (see Appendix B of this book). Posters too became attractive, clear and encouraging: "Can't afford your fuel bills? It has been so cold lately you may be able to get help with your fuel bills". At the time, Donnison (1982, p 230) welcomed "simpler clearer leaflets, forms and posters".

These apparent contradictions within the New Right philosophy illustrate that making policy is not a straightforward process. It is determined by many and often contradictory influences. How can these improvements in overall information provision be explained within what had become a policy of targeting? Are they after all evidence of a commitment to improve access to all benefits, or perhaps of inertia, an information machine simply rolling on, regardless of wider policy aims?

More evidence from the early 1980s of a shift to targeted publicity and information seem to show that the two examples discussed earlier were exceptions. In response to a suggestion that a copy of 'Which Benefit?' – now a free leaflet with brief details of all financial help from the department – be sent to every household in the UK, a minister at the DHSS, Lynda Chalker, declined to do so:

> The great majority would be delivered to households where residents would not be entitled to any benefits, or where they are already receiving their full entitlements. I believe that it is better to concentrate on specialised publicity aimed at particularly vulnerable groups. The forthcoming press and television campaign for family income supplement aimed at low income working families is an example of this. (*Hansard*, 10 November 1980, col 66)

Targeting of publicity means making choices about what not to publicise and, therefore, about who will – and will not – be informed. This is contrary to the rhetoric and spirit of the 1980 Act and to the ideals of social democratic rights. It is evident, however, that other considerations had long been influencing information policy.

The 1980s were also the heyday of pressure groups. They made access to welfare benefits possible for many people who were otherwise ignorant of their rights. The Social Security Advisory Committee (SSAC), which had replaced the SBC, welcomed what it perceived as the trend by claimants to regard benefits as rights. However the SSAC concluded that there was still a clear responsibility on the department and that there was room for improvement:

It would be a gross distortion to represent the majority of people claiming social security benefits as being well-informed and advised.... We know that Ministers and officials put considerable emphasis on maintaining and improving the quality of social security leaflets. We should like to see leaflets more generally displayed and available, both in local offices, post offices and in less traditional outlets such as public libraries, doctors' surgeries, places of work and so on. The leaflets must of course be up to date ... provision of good clear information is essential. (SSAC, 1982, p 57)

Other evidence of information policy in the 1980s supports the view that there had been a shift in policy. Placing the onus on claimants to find out for themselves and of a more passive rather than active government fits with the Conservative perspective on citizenship. This change had already been detected in 1979, and there is evidence to support a continuing trend. Walker and Walker (1987) comment on a shift in attitude and in administrative procedures, a change described by them as a system of 'do-it-yourself social security'. Two senior officials involved at that time put it this way:

"I think the previous [Conservative] government's position was that the material was available and it was up to you to find it.... I think for the previous government, the information was there, if you are entitled you can claim, and that was as far as they were going to take it."

"The previous [Conservative] government's position was more one of not being too energetic in this area [people claiming their entitlements] rather than deliberately overlooking it."

Although there was a clear shift away from the social democratic 'inclusive' ideal to the targeting of information, there were some positive, if cautious, reactions to the government's efforts. For example, Deacon and Bradshaw (1983, p 140) point out that, while "the amount of effort varies from benefit to benefit", there was "a steady effort made by central government and local authorities to provide basic knowledge about the availability of benefits". Bradshaw (1985, p 108) in particular applauds the Conservative government's efforts to make means testing work by being prepared to spend on information and publicity (although he acknowledges that non-take-up is an inherent problem):

Between 1979/80 and 1983/84, the DHSS spent £98,000 on advertising SB [Supplementary Benefit], £1.6 million on FIS [Family Income Support] and £760,000 on HB [Housing Benefit]. These are trivial amounts compared with the level of expenditure on benefits; but they do indicate that the government is not entirely unconcerned about the problem of take-up.

(See Appendix A of this book to put these figures into context.)

The Child Poverty Action Group (CPAG) also gives the government some credit for its provision of information. However,

> On the negative side, it seems unlikely that a government as committed to reducing public spending as the present one would conduct a serious take-up effort in the knowledge that it would thereby increase public spending. (CPAG, nd, p 4)

The tension between rising expenditure on social security and promoting benefits had been recognised from the start of the welfare state. That tension was highlighted by a local authority take-up campaign in Strathclyde in 1982. Faced with the possible loss by local claimants of benefits worth in the region of £1 million, the council sent out 100,000 envelopes containing postcards inviting claims for benefits. The postcards were to be sent by residents direct to the DHSS and, if the claims were successful, take-up of benefits would increase before the regulations changed. This was a local policy critical of central government:

> The campaign was political dynamite. Poor Lynda Chalker [a Minister at the DHSS] was caught trying to maintain a rhetorical commitment to take-up while as a minister of a cutting government, obstructing the Strathclyde campaign. It was an untenable position, as the Press was quick to let her know. (Sharron, 1982, p 8)

For a minister to publicly move away from the rhetoric of rights would be politically dangerous. However, a politician involved at the time expressed his condemnation in a different way:

> "There were one or two take-up campaigns which were really very counter-productive. The local social security office was suddenly completely inundated, apart from a drop in morale as they contemplated these heaps.... I genuinely did not think that was a very helpful or sensible thing to do."

The Minister for Social Security, Tony Newton, was more explicit about the administrative implications. In the House of Commons he said, "We are in charge and we believe that the present torrent of claims could cause the breakdown of the entire social security system" (*Hansard*, 23 July 1986, col 444). Pressure on administrative resources may have been uppermost in his mind, but the inevitable loss of rights was not lost on the opposition, which defended the campaign.

> The fact is that those welfare rights claims are purely to ensure that people get what the House has said they are entitled to claim.... It is wrong to suggest that the social security system depends on a massive failure to take-up benefits.... A right is acceptable to Conservative Members as long as it is

not taken up by too many people. The omens are ominous for future
attempts to improve take-up of benefits. (*Hansard*, 23 July 1986, col 445 and
446)

The aimed-for simplicity of the 1980 Act, intended to make it easier for potential
claimants to understand their rights, was not achieved. Ditch (1993) recognises
the need for better information as one of the problems of the DHSS in the
1980s. Welfare rights workers enabled many citizens to receive their entitlements.
Their campaigns also brought to public attention general areas of concern
about the social security scheme including the effectiveness of government
information provision and government attitudes to the citizenship status of
many groups.

The Secretary of State for Social Services, Norman Fowler, established a
review of the system in 1984. This was partly in response to successful campaigns
by non-government agencies on behalf of claimants (Walker, 1986). Yet again,
the review was portrayed as a quest for a simpler system that could increase
take-up levels. The Green Paper seemed clear:

The Government's proposals for reform of the benefit system set a high
premium on greater simplicity…. People should be able to know what help
they can get. (Green Paper, 1985a, p 43)

It cannot be right to run a system which required claimants to have such a
detailed knowledge in order to get their entitlement. (Green Paper, 1985b,
p 18)

One politician involved at the time agreed that this would be a positive step:

"The Tory government's way of tackling the problem of information about
a complex system was to simplify the system. It made a big difference when
claimants were clearer about their entitlements. There was no longer
discretion and the system was easier to understand."

The 1988 legislation would replace Supplementary Benefit with Income
Support, additional weekly payments, lump sum grants with premiums for
particular groups and with social fund loans. The minister commented on the
simplicity of the new scheme: "Social security is no longer a jungle of files and
paper where only the skilled claimant triumphs" (Fowler, 1991, p 224).

Dean (1991), however, detects other explanations for the proposed changes.
The new scheme although simpler would reduce levels of benefit for many
claimants. The government wanted to cut public spending and there was
pressure from right-wing Conservatives to allow the welfare state to wither
away. The system had also become impossible to administer. According to a
leaked memorandum, the DHSS attempted to 'postpone or change' a Channel
4 television campaign advertising welfare benefits planned for February 1987,

because it would involve too much extra work for DHSS offices (*Guardian*, 28 February 1987).

Cook (1989, p 123) detects additional and more worrying shifts concerning attitudes to social rights:

> Government's ambivalence to improving benefit take-up can be regarded by some as a pragmatic response to burgeoning public expenditure on social security and the desire to promote an unwillingness to rely on state welfare. This may ultimately lead to a situation in which 'entitlement' to benefit means little.

Other observers agree that expenditure was *the* crucial influence on social security and information policy at that time. One senior officer in a voluntary agency expressed the view that:

> "They did not really have a philosophy, or a grand plan. They were driven to think about it. Someone looked at the budget and said 'My god, look at these costs. We must do something'."

One politician was similarly forthright in his opinion:

> "Well of course the Tories were never in favour of doing it [publicity to increase take-up] because all it would do would be increase the budget for social security if they were successful in promotional take-up campaigns. Encouraging people to test their eligibility would cost them a lot of money. So it's rather understandable that they had nothing to do with it."

Attempts to simplify the system must therefore be seen in the wider political and economic context. This was a government aiming to 'roll back the state', to reduce social security expenditure, and to ease the administrative problems of the system. Policies needed to reduce dependence on benefits while at the same time avoid the appearance of denying claimants their rights. This difficult balancing act, demonstrating again that making policy is not straightforward, was reflected in the Conservative government's apparently contradictory policies. Laurance's (1987b, p 23) observation is reminiscent of Glennerster's comment in 1962, mentioned in Chapter Four:

> The DHSS's view is that its responsibility is merely to *pay* the benefits.... History shows the government jumping first one way then the other on social security: publicising a benefit and then cutting it back. It never seems sure how many claimants it *wants* to get what they are entitled to. (emphasis in original)

Income support from 1988

Major changes to the benefit scheme had an impact on information policy. One voluntary agency officer remembered:

> "It did change in 1988. The onus was shifted back on to the claimant because less information was needed.... It was made simpler.... Its prime purpose was cost cutting and simplicity, simplicity of administration."

A politician expressed it this way:

> "Part of the thinking behind simplifying the system in 1986 was of course to get away from the situation, or to reduce the extent to which, the sheer complexity of the system at the worst made it almost impossible for people to work out what their entitlement was. So that however much wish there was for people to claim their entitlement it was a tangle through which even quite well-informed people could hardly find their way. Complexity arose from the difficulty that even the people operating the system found it quite difficult to understand."

A senior official described another aspect of the change:

> "It was not quite a sea change, but a move change if you like, that has grown since, more from SB to IS that started it, there was a kind of feeling that because you applied for SB, 'Can I have it please?' was almost the attitude, you were an applicant, whereas when IS came in it was an entitlement. It was underpinned by regulations and that started a change in attitude and ethos."

There were other issues, however, which clouded the picture for information policy. In addition to simplification, the new scheme continued a trend which "confirmed means-testing as the central feature of social security" (Alcock, 1990, p 90). Means testing brings all the inherent problems of ignorance and low take-up, and, therefore, the additional need for information if claimants are to exercise their rights. It is inimical to simplification. Davies and Ritchie (quoted in Alcock et al, 1991, p 58) notice different shifts in government attitude:

> They [the Department of Social Security] present the problem now as individual claimants' reluctance to claim benefit, rather than a lack of accessible information; and suggest persuasive personal counselling as the solution, rather than publicity campaigns.

Counselling implies the need for claimants to change *their* attitude to receiving benefits. This could be made more difficult at a time when government attitudes were seen as a "discouragement of any positive images of claimant status via an enhanced policing role within benefit administration" (Alcock, 1990, p 91). Another official recollected that the Conservatives:

> "did not want to run national advertising campaigns because they thought there was enough advice about benefits generally available from the Benefits Agency."

Cook (1989) offers another explanation. She attributes a lack of information provision to political ideologies and inequalities of power. Supporting the now familiar themes of limitations on resources, both administrative and financial, she observes that a "lack of knowledge on the part of benefit claimants may be seen as essential in order to render an increasingly unworkable system workable" (Cook, 1989, p 124). Recognising the gap between government rhetoric and the reality, she comments that an *apparent* policy aim to encourage claims "was subverted by the latent policy goal of cutting government expenditure" (Cook, 1989, p 21).

Evidence of the lack of information for 16- and 17-year-olds entitled to discretionary hardship payments in the early 1990s illustrates some of these interwoven issues. A member of The Coalition on Young People and Social Security (COYPSS, 1999, personal communication) described what happened at the time:

> "We were trying to encourage the BA to mount an awareness campaign and there was some sense that they were open to the idea but it seemed that perhaps the policy initiative at that time was to do nothing which would increase the numbers of young people claiming.... The government should have provided information but they were not prepared to foot the bill. Bureaucracy is devised to deter claims and reduce expenditure. Legislation is a mechanism for social control. They think that if payments are made lots of young people will leave home."

A senior official involved confirmed that there had been a proposal for such a campaign, but remembered that "It was soundly squashed then by the Treasury ... it was abandoned because of the budget situation". Another official, talking in more general terms, agreed with this view:

> "The [Benefit] Agency ran up against this diktat by the Treasury ... who were concerned about the increase in expenditure.... Very seldom did they run benefit take-up campaigns for that reason."

It is evidently the case also that the Treasury's financial decisions reflect their (implicit) attitudes to particular social policies (Deakin and Parry, 1998) and to a wider political agenda. Fears of a right-wing backlash should benefits be paid to middle-class young people and of a government appearing to condone young people leaving home may have been the major determinants of a politically expedient information policy. This complex mix of issues outweighed the information – and financial – needs of eligible 16- and 17-year-olds.

In the early 1990s, however, an active and very successful campaign was mounted to publicise and promote Disability Living Allowance (DLA). Judged by government information policies up to that time, attitudes to disabled people – and therefore to their status as citizens – had been at best ambivalent. As a group, they had been variously ignored or sought out for special treatment. However, they were becoming an increasingly vocal campaigning lobby (Oliver, 1990; Drake, 1999). One senior official explained the campaign as a way "to buy off the disability lobby prior to, or to avoid, the Disability Discrimination Act.... Ministers wanted a huge result". There was a 47% increase in claims for DLA between 1993 and 1996, which was officially attributed to a much greater awareness of the benefit (DSS, 2000b). In a twist that again demonstrates that making policy is a complex process, and where results are not always predictable, 'success' brought its own problems: the administration of the system was overwhelmed; there were long delays in processing claims; allegations of abuse were levelled against some claimants, resulting later in the 'integrity project' to check eligibility of all claimants of higher rates of DLA. As one senior official remembered, there were lessons to be learned from the campaign:

> "Part of what determines how much something is promoted is what can the BA actually cope with ... in the disability campaign we did over-stimulate the market."

A welfare rights worker suspected political reasons for the campaign and also witnessed the failure of the administration to cope with unexpected success:

> "DLA was heavily publicised in 1992 ... lots of people could get the new benefits. It was [Prime Minister] Major's government and an election year.... It was a shock to BA when claims increased dramatically and they are wary since of publicity about changes ... they just got swamped."

This 'success' raises questions about what can be defined as 'effective' publicity and about how to anticipate and respond to the demands that such campaigns stimulate. Clearly, lack of administrative or other resources should not be a reason for denying rights, although this is a familiar situation for other welfare services such as health, personal social services and housing. One politician, recalling the 1992 campaign, agreed that success was difficult to define:

> "Clearly judged on the basis of take-up the campaign for DLA has been successful to the point at which numbers of people think it needs to be curbed. The system was overloaded or under-resourced depending on which way you look at it.... It becomes questionable whether you would be wise to try to stimulate that demand still further."

In contrast to their 'bad' experience of DLA, government ministers went ahead with improvements in the claim forms and leaflets to promote another benefit for disabled people, Attendance Allowance (AA). This was an expensive benefit but, according to one senior official involved at the time, policy makers were convinced by research showing that claimants tended to die very quickly after receiving it. Higher take-up would not therefore prove expensive in the longer term. This would be a popular move, unlikely to attract abuse or public condemnation.

The National Audit Office Report of 1988 (NAO, 1988), while acknowledging the department's efforts, contained both praise and criticism of its provision of information. It urged better and more effective information and publicity. Others agreed that there was room for improvement:

> Although glossy TV adverts and free telephone helplines heralded the birth of Income Support in April 1988, a bewildering lack of hard information on the 'simplified' new scheme generated confusion and anxiety for claimants and DHSS staff alike. (*Welfare Rights Bulletin*, 1988)

Attitudes to informing potential claimants at this time are unclear. Even though the 1988 legislation emphasised rights, information policies often resulted in targeting and cost cutting. These choices were themselves based on value judgements about claimants' rights and therefore their citizenship status. A chilling comment from a senior official confirms this:

> "I can't remember anyone ever wanting to encourage people to claim income support. IS and SB were not pushed because they could not afford for them to be pushed. That was explicit within the Department ... we were [also] endlessly trying to get improved marketing for health benefits. It was absolutely 'no, no' and the administrative costs were very high ... just not the kind of thing one can do."

In contrast to the contradictory policies detailed above, however, there is evidence that in the early 1990s the (now) Department of Social Security (DSS) embarked "on a more structured communications strategy in their literature ... the overall aim was to make social security easier to understand and more accessible" (Corden, 1995, p 29). Others also applauded the DSS's ongoing efforts (Perkins et al, 1991). The departmental report published in 1989 (DSS, 1989) gave details for the first time of the DSS's expenditure on paid media publicity and advertising (see Appendix A of this book). The DSS certainly continued in their annual reports of the 1990s to emphasise their own continuing efforts to provide information, which were explicitly linked at this time to levels of take-up of benefit. It acknowledged that a significant proportion of people who are eligible do not claim. Confirming a shift earlier described as 'do-it-yourself social security', the DSS was also explicit about the limits of its responsibility for information provision:

The Department's policy on take-up is to ensure that members of the public have ready access to comprehensive, accurate and comprehensible information about benefit entitlement.... The Department tries to ensure claimants are in a position to make informed choices on whether to claim ... social security legislation clearly places the onus of claiming on individuals. (DSS, 1990, p 13)

Organisational changes were to complicate the picture even more for information policy. Bellamy and Henderson (1992, p 3) explain the changes as "a response to ideological shifts associated with the rise of the New Right". The introduction in 1991 of 'Next Steps' agencies resulted in most operational tasks being transferred from the DSS to the BA (Ling, 1994; Butcher, 1995). Both, however, had explicit aims to provide information (DSS, 1994; BA, 1995a) and had budgets for that purpose. It was inevitable that there would be some confusion with regard to information policy as a result. One senior official described the "DSS/BA demarcation between policy making and implementation as a bit fuzzy", what Greer (1994, p 67) describes as an "obfuscation of responsibilities".

The changes were also confusing for claimants. However, a definite change to a more positive attitude to information provision was remembered by a senior official working in the new agency at that time:

"I certainly think that the change, the introduction of executive agencies and the formation of BA has also made quite a change from our point of view inside, if you like, which has also spread like a ripple effect outside. There is much more emphasis on the customer service angle ... it's much more customer oriented."

This is confirmed by Corden (1995, p 26), who observes that the "DSS/Benefits Agency now have a strong commitment to communication and information strategies". However, despite the rhetoric and good intentions, one of the explicit reasons for the change was 'value for money'. One senior official spelled out the consequences for claimants:

"There was a sea change really about 1995 whereby customer service became an expensive option which ministers did not smile upon."

Walker and Brittain (1995, p 30), looking at it from the perspective of the claimant, notice a now familiar theme:

The view that the Benefits Agency and its staff have a vested interest in minimising expenditure seems still to be widespread among the Agency's customers.... Improving the quality of the Agency's advice and information services may well increase the level of demand.

The Secretary of State did not set targets for the BA to provide information, or goals for take-up of benefits (Greer, 1994). Ditch (1993) regards this as a notable omission, and one that undermines the credibility of the BA among both claimants and advice workers. Absence of a target does not necessarily mean that the DSS and BA are not able, or keen, to go on improving their information provision. It does, however, require resources. An officer in a voluntary agency described the situation thus:

> "The concentration of the agencies on what they see as their core tasks, which is not about out-reach and all that, has changed the ethos over time. Since the BA came in 1991 with a much higher profile, a much more explicit ethos and did win a lot of trust and definitely did try to improve things. There was an attempt to be more customer orientated, trying to shift the culture. It never went as far as anyone wanted but there has definitely been a change, a retrenchment from that, partly to do with enormous resource pressures and a definition of their key task which was to deliver benefit to existing customers."

Two officials confirmed the low status of publicity and information within overall budgets. Publicity, they said, "was way down in their [policy makers'] considerations of how things should be" and "is the most vulnerable part of the DSS budget when running costs are tight". Such low priority could be expected to result in less information about *all* benefits. Any exceptions to a policy of retrenchment can help to understand attitudes to the citizenship status of particular groups of claimants.

'Freeline', the innovative telephone information service, was mentioned earlier in this chapter as an example of information policy that seemed to be at variance with the general ethos of targeting information. 'Freeline' was described as a surprising innovation in 1984 by a Conservative government aiming to cut back on social security. Moodie (1988, p 5) called it a "super initiative which has proved a great success". By 1995, it was answering over 3,250,000 calls each year, making it the largest provider of social security information (*Welfare Rights Bulletin*, 1996a). That same year, the BA reported improvements to the service and pledged that the staff "will continue to strive for increased customer satisfaction" (BA, 1995b, p 12).

'Freeline' closed on 12 July 1996. The official justification for closure was a 'rationalisation' of services. It was decided that the service duplicated rather than complemented local office services and was limited by the lack of computer access to personal records. One senior official explained it this way:

> "When ['Freeline'] was closed, the decision was taken partly on cost grounds, and also because it was not the most efficient way of providing a service. Its particular limitation was that it could not provide information on individual cases. You could never get information on a particular case."

The unions challenged the official figure of £28 million that would be saved over five years. The closure was also criticised for lack of consultation and lack of advanced warning. It was said to "defy logic" (*Welfare Rights Bulletin*, 1996a, p 5) by practitioners who saw the closure as a clear denial of rights, bringing only limited financial savings.

Reaction to the closure was mixed. Many saw the service as a vital and successful method of providing information to the public. The final irony for them was the launch of the National Fraud hotline on 5 August 1996 – only one month after the closure of 'Freeline' – with a publicity budget of £500,000 (*Welfare Rights Bulletin*, 1996b). Within the DSS, some officials greeted the way the changeover was handled with dismay, as these two comments show:

> "That was a presentational disaster really, and opening the fraud line. They are the first to admit it. 'It could have been better', I think they would go as far as saying, but it was a disaster really. I think it was coincidental, but it was badly planned at the very least."

> "That was a major change whereby they changed the telephone lines, with these poor staff sitting on them, who had actually been providing the responses to general enquiries and that was the same staff. Freeline stopped and that line went immediately over to fraud. Talk about culture shock!"

However, the shift in policy fitted with the Conservative's overall agenda, including a definition of citizenship that placed more emphasis on responsibilities. Deakin and Parry (2000, p 124) observe that fraud had become "an increasing pre-occupation under Peter Lilley", Secretary of State for Social Security from 1992 to 1997. During that time, information campaigns began to encourage the public to inform on people they suspected of benefit fraud. "Publicity has been a key component in the success of the [fraud] hotline" (DSS press release, 7 August 1997, 97/151). One senior official described the Conservative's action on fraud as "part of a much more philosophical approach to rights and responsibilities". Lister (1998b, p 317) comments that "Citizenship responsibility is invoked even more explicitly in relation to social security fraud". The consequence of an increasing emphasis on fraud was "much less attention is paid to under-claiming" (Johnson, 1990, p 225). A Treasury official confirms this shifting emphasis:

> We have agreed with the DSS extra resources to go into fraud and we have ring-fenced it, which means that the deal is that they don't direct any of that money that we've allocated to fraud to other things like marketing leaflets [*laughter*]. (Deakin and Parry, 2000, p 125; emphasis in original)

The issues of fraud and low take-up were inextricably linked. For example, the decision in 1996 to close 'Freeline' had been anticipated in a debate on benefit fraud in the House of Commons in March that year, in which several MPs raised the question of low take-up:

> The other side of the coin, which is equally important, is take-up of and entitlement to benefit. When attempting to root out fraud, the Government should apply the same effort and commitment to ensuring that those who are eligible for benefit receive their entitlement.... I hope that the government will tell us tonight that they will launch new publicity drives. (*Hansard*, 5 March 1996, col 236)

What the Conservative government did launch was their 'Change' programme, aiming to modernise the administration, and to improve accuracy and security (Social Security Advisory Committee, 1997). It cut the BA's budget by over £200 million and the department's operating costs by 25% over three years (Sainsbury, 1998). It was to "threaten the very nature of the organisation, its culture and its working policies" (Hadwen, 1997, p 11). There were political and financial reasons for the cuts, and "The Treasury now became fed up with social security" (Deakin and Parry, 2000, p 115).

Inevitably there would be implications yet again for claimants. "Some offices indicated that the freeze on budgets had already meant that customer services had been reduced" (Social Security Advisory Committee, 1997, p 10). The impact on information policy and provision was clear:

> Claimants [could be] less likely to apply for benefits in the first place due to lack of information about their entitlement and difficulty of access to the BA. (Hadwen, 1997, p 13)

One senior official demonstrated that the difficulties were also all too real for staff:

> "As an agency we've had to cut our costs by 25% over three years.... It's difficult then to relate trying to increase take-up for people while we're running down our costs. How do we get the two to go together?... It's one big contradiction."

Allbeson (1997) confirms the shifts in policy and agrees that claimants would be the losers:

> During the last nine months the Benefits Agency has retreated significantly from its 'enabling' role of ensuring that members of the public are informed of their entitlements to benefit and that all claimants have access to its services on an equal footing. (1997, p 1)

> It is a sign of how far the Benefits Agency has moved away from its original objective of providing comprehensive information to the public on social

security benefits that asking the Benefits Agency for detailed, accurate advice about benefit entitlements can now be an exceedingly hit and miss affair. (1997, p 12)

... the claimant's perspective features very little in any of them ['Change' projects], the principle aim being an improved service for the people who run it rather than the people who use it. (1997, p 21)

Summary

From 1979, the government continued earlier shifts away from social democratic ideals. Information policy reflected wider political and economic issues, but under the Conservatives it reflected also a fundamental change in political philosophy and values. Policy was influenced by political expedience and by a desire to reduce dependency on the state. Consequently limited resources were committed to publicity and information. The aim of a simplified scheme where people could easily find out for themselves was not realised.

The complexity of policy making and ambivalence about objectives are illustrated by contradictions in information policy. The tension between promoting benefits and reducing costs is evident throughout this period, although for some observers there was no tension. They detected a deliberate aim to reduce the ability of some citizens to exercise their rights, based on political, resource or moral grounds. For other claimants there were successful campaigns. Increased targeting of benefit information and successful campaigns coexisted with some effective provision about all benefits. Despite these contradictions, information policy clearly reflected a redefinition of citizenship, altering the balance between rights and responsibilities.

SIX

New Labour and information

New Labour came to power in 1997 under the leadership of Tony Blair. There was an expectation of fundamental changes following 18 years of Conservative government. The welfare state, which "in its present form is neither sustainable nor desirable" (Sainsbury, 1998, p 123) would need radical reform "to make it responsive to the altered circumstances in which we live today" (Giddens, 1998, p 20). The 'Third Way' political perspective (Blair, 1998) is sometimes unclear, ambiguous or unpredictable (Powell, 1999), causing uncertainties about the direction, policies and values of the new government. There is, however, a complex mixture of policy change and policy continuity – both with 'Old Labour' (though few) and with the Conservatives. This is also an explicitly 'populist' government.

There was a commitment from the start to accept Conservative spending plans until 1999 (Bochel and Bochel, 1998; Burchardt and Hills, 1999). The tension between ever-increasing demands on resources and promoting benefits would be difficult to resolve for a government pledged not to increase social spending and, at the same time, be inclusive and 'open'. It was also said that this was a Treasury with the implicit conceptualisation of social security as the "bills of economic and social failure" (Deakin and Parry, 2000, p 180).

The implication of the 'Third Way' for information would seem to be a shift away from the social democratic paternalism of 'Old Labour' and from the party's traditional emphasis on social rights. With a redefined relationship between individuals and the state, an active government would expect to inform citizens of their rights, their responsibilities and their opportunities (Blair, 1998; Greenaway, 1998). In turn, citizens would be expected to be more active in exploring opportunities (Williams, 1999) and meeting their own welfare needs. How far would this be reflected in information policies? Is it possible to detect attitudes to citizenship in New Labour's approach to information and the promotion of welfare – and from social policies themselves? This chapter gives examples of policy change, of continuity and of innovation.

A hopeful and early sign of change in 1997 was the reversal of the Conservative's intention to close all Benefits Agency (BA) offices in Wales. The consequences of doing so would have been severe in many ways, not least in terms of providing a source of information to claimants. One senior official noticed a general shift to a more proactive information policy:

> "The line then, before 1997, was that we publicise benefits but it was peoples' responsibility to claim benefits to which they were entitled. Now I have gone on to the other side of the fence. This change of ethos has been since

the last government came in. It is a policy change, but the BA are reacting to it."

There is rhetoric to support the new approach. The Secretary of State for Social Security, Harriet Harman, launched the 'Active Modern Service' approach in December 1997. One of its principles was a 'Customer Focus', "to provide one-stop service, giving people information and access to secure their rights" (DSS, 1998a, p 29). The departmental report of 1998 (DSS, 1998a) acknowledges the failure of the existing system to give information in an accessible form. The Citizen's Charter committed the Department of Social Security (DSS) and its agencies to "providing full, accurate information in plain language about services" (DSS, 1998a, p 46). The charter was relaunched in 1998 as the 'Service First' programme, committing the DSS and its agencies to "be open and provide full information" (DSS, 1999, p 34).

One politician confirmed the rhetoric in these documents and a shift that distanced the new government from the previous administration. Any tension between promoting benefits and the need to economise on social security spending was denied:

> "The previous government, I think, just did not want to let people know what their rights were, and if they did not claim, tough, we make a saving.... They felt that the best model of welfare was to make it as unpleasant as possible, as incomprehensible as possible and drive as many people away from going anywhere near a BA office as they possibly could.... We don't see it like that. We think people are entitled to the benefits parliament has said they are entitled to and it's up to us to get them delivered as quickly as possible.... I just don't see that there's a tension there."

A senior official also confirmed the intention to make information more effective:

> "I do believe that part of the difficulty that the department had in the past is because it is faceless, it did not have any sort of personality.... What you can do I think through good communications is hope people will respect you as an organisation because you are genuinely trying to help them with their rights and responsibilities. All our public campaigns are planned around that tenet."

Ditch (1999, p 6) suggests reasons for this apparently new approach:

> The in-coming Labour government were keen to make an early impact in the field of social security but were aware of the need to advance cautiously. Policy pronouncements, initiatives and innovative pilot projects all found their way on to the agenda while, at the same time a (supposedly) more radical/fundamental review of policy was undertaken.

However, there are practices that show New Labour accepting and continuing policies embarked on by its predecessor that would be detrimental to the exercise of rights. It continued with the 'Change' programme (see Chapter Five of this book), which aimed to modernise and improve the service. By cutting operating costs, the programme inevitably reduced customer services and constrained the provision of information for all claimants. A few months after the election victory, New Labour also enacted the 1997 Social Security (Claims and Payments) Regulations. Regulations Four and Six mark an important shift to making claimants responsible for providing information to support their claim. Information to potential claimants *by* the DSS/BA has to be matched by information from claimants *to* the DSS/BA. Failure to do so means that the claim will not be decided upon and claimants will lose benefit (Sainsbury, 1998). This is a measure designed to reduce administration costs. It requires claimants to be more active and, although not directly affecting information policy, was perceived as shifting the balance of responsibility. The BA Business Plan for 1998/99, in a section entitled 'Better Information', is clear about what is expected of customers as citizens:

> We have already revised claim forms and leaflets so that customers know what their responsibilities are when it comes to providing all the facts for determining their entitlement to benefit. We expect customers to provide the necessary information honestly and promptly. (BA, 1998, p 9)

The third example concerns the legacy of the successful promotion of benefits for disabled people, which itself unwittingly became a campaign. The 1992 campaign to promote Disability Living Allowance (DLA) (see Chapter Five of this book), had overwhelmed the administration. It prompted suspicions of abuse and an 'integrity' project to check the eligibility of claimants of higher rates of the benefit. New Labour threatened to cut disability benefits. The threat was seen as a clear statement of government attitudes towards the status of disabled people and their rights. This 'bad news' attracted a lot of media attention and publicity. The disability lobby organised public demonstrations (Daniel, 1998) and 65 Labour MPs voted against the proposals in the 1999 Welfare Reform Bill. An officer in a voluntary agency explained how it was perceived:

> "It was pointed out that 'getting the right money to the right person' – did not that also mean that we knew there were a large percentage getting less than the right amount? They did not have an answer to that. That was quite explicitly not what the integrity project was about. It's clearly about money."

A senior official disagreed and thought the integrity project had been misconstrued:

> "The extremely bad publicity that attached itself to the disability benefit review, the integrity project, which was just supposed to be a review, became a kind of fraud exercise in everybody's mind … a wolf in sheep's clothing."

The 'integrity' project ceased at the end of March 1999.

An expensive campaign to promote pensions made it clear that New Labour, again following a policy of the previous administration, expected people to take more responsibility for their own futures. This provides another example of the importance under New Labour of the responsibilities of citizenship and of government attempts to educate the public. If successful, it would also reduce future social security expenditure. One senior official described the aim of the campaign, which cost £1,275,000 in 1997/98, thus:

> "There's a campaign to encourage more people to start thinking at an early age that they need to have an additional pension. The basic state pension will not be enough for them to live on when they retire … people have a poor grasp of this on the whole…. What we are trying to do is give people some knowledge about the sorts of pensions there are and what the different terms mean … so the campaign is trying gently to help them to take some control."

In contrast, another initiative inherited by the government seems to support the concept of citizenship rights rather than responsibilities. New Labour continued with 'Project Access', an initiative to overhaul all social security leaflets. It aimed to make it easier for all claimants to know their rights. The Social Security Minister Keith Bradley explained:

> I am asking the Benefits Agency to simplify its leaflets, in order to provide better information and allow the customer easier access to the benefits system. New leaflets will be designed with the customer as the main focus, not the system. Fewer, but more user friendly, leaflets will allow customers to assess their eligibility to benefits better, and so access the social security system more effectively. This will represent a radical improvement in customer service…. A better informed customer will help us pay the right money, to the right person, at the right time, every time. (DSS Press Release, 17 November 1997, 97/247)

'Project Access' was based on the results of research and consultation started under the Conservative government in 1995. It shows a planned policy with a clear purpose and tangible results. The new leaflets were phased in over 18 months. The BA "concluded that we had got it about right. The leaflets have sent a clear message to customers that we are making information more accessible" (BA, 2000, p 14).

There was support for the initiative from those directly involved in the service. One senior official involved commented:

"I think there was a general recognition that what we were doing was not really meeting the needs of the people who wanted information. The feedback we were getting from our DINOs [District Information Officers] and such like was that the leaflet programme needed an overhaul."

A politician expressed enthusiasm for the project:

"We've been revamping the incomprehensible sort of leaflets and I think we have come up with something that is much better. We've reduced the number.... These things just grow like topsy if you don't viciously cut them back now and then.... Hopefully people will find them more easily usable. We're clearly looking to see what we can do across the entire system to make that kind of switch from a jargonised sort of massive numbers of available confusions to something that is more easily accessible."

Others working with claimants, however, had doubts about the project, based on the BA's reliance on – and approach to – leaflets. Officers of voluntary organisations expressed their views thus:

"The task of providing information in an accessible form is actually quite a sophisticated job that needs proper resources allocated to it. That's only a tiny part of the process because it does not even begin to get at people who don't pick up leaflets in post offices."

"However good the leaflets are they have to be backed up by staff that know not just the benefit but have a general overview and that does not seem to happen very often because there's a huge turnover. I think they realise they have too many leaflets, that's one thing. It's far too complicated and they've got leaflets that repeat each other and leaflets that are subsets of other leaflets and so on."

"Obviously the DSS and BA provide quite a lot of information and have made quite a lot of effort to improve these [new leaflets] as well. People don't like the covers, they give out the wrong message."

A local authority welfare rights worker was even more concerned:

"For the public, the new leaflets are hopeless. The idea is better but the result is not an improvement.... It's difficult to be wrong if you are vague and incomplete.... On our open day we considered taking them off display in case people took them and read them."

These comments on 'Project Access' confirm some of the difficulties of providing information, however well intentioned and committed politicians and civil servants are. However, more worrying is the fact that research into sources of information and claiming behaviour (see Chapter Three of this book) provides ample evidence that leaflets are not an effective way of informing potential claimants about their entitlements (see also NAO, 1988; Vincent et al, 1995; Cummins, 1996; Stafford et al, 1996). This must cast doubt on the potential effectiveness of 'Project Access' and consequently on the extent to which government really did want to make it easier for people to claim their rights.

New Labour has also been innovative in the way benefits are promoted. The Prime Minister embarked on a 'welfare roadshow', touring the country to explain why welfare reform was necessary. This was a high-level exercise in media management in preparation for the publication of 'New Ambitions for Our Country' (Green Paper, 1998). It was prompted by several issues, including: anger among MPs at cuts in rates of child benefit for lone parents; the perceived need to be seen to be tough on benefit fraud; and a desire to stress the new emphasis on responsibilities.

Fairclough (2000) comments that the Green Paper was itself promotional, 'oscillating' between 'telling and selling' rather than a basis for discussion and debate.

The Chancellor's 'surprise' announcement in 1997 of winter fuel payments was another innovation in both benefit and information policy (Deakin and Parry, 1998). A new scheme to provide extra money to all pensioners was a departure from previous forms of assistance. It certainly made an impact and was warmly welcomed by older people and groups working with them. The strategic importance to the government of this 'good news' policy was evident from the high level of commitment to the scheme and from the cost of the publicity campaign of £1.7 million (see Appendix A of this book to put this figure into context). One politician observed:

> "The Treasury are now coming up with the ideas.... All the policy is coming
> out of the Treasury ... it is full of whizz-bang ideas."

The campaign was, however, criticised. It was argued that it was not necessary to promote payments that would be made automatically without the need to make a claim. The Minister justified the expense by responding that pensioners needed to be reassured about their entitlement (*Hansard*, 26 January 1998, col 15). The campaign was also alleged to be contrary to a recommendation by civil servants that it was a party political advertising campaign.

The government was keen to be seen to be doing something for older people. They had made promises in their 1997 manifesto (Labour Party, 1997a) and clearly thought that this publicity would demonstrate their commitment. However, the campaign did prompt criticism from those who regard only a rise in retirement pensions as the equitable way to treat pensioners and restore their status as full citizens. Publicity about winter fuel payments was seen as a way to deflect attention from more fundamental issues. There are echoes here of Laurance's curiosity about the timing of a new leaflet to explain help with heating costs a decade earlier. He surmises that "perhaps the government is simply trying to distract attention from other more important, and more chaotic, areas of its policy making" (Laurance, 1987a, p 20).

Two comments, the first from a politician and the second from an officer in a voluntary organisation, agree with Laurance:

> "A recent example of government effort to actively publicise a new benefit is winter fuel payments. The reasons for the publicity are political, a new benefit, for the government to get credit and to head off the recent debate within Labour about increases in pensions rising in line with prices not earnings ... publicity about particular benefits helps to ensure the success of a policy."

> "The decisions made by the DSS about the provision of information, that's very interesting, because I get the feeling that they publicise things that look good. Because it's something they feel is media friendly and looks good they are very active on that.... When it's something unpleasant, generalising hugely, it does seem to be the case that the details come out later."

The timing of the Chancellor's 'good news' announcement of winter fuel payments coincided with media publicity about the 'bad news' of cuts in lone-parent benefits. This latter proposal was widely criticised in the media and by the Social Security Advisory Committee (Deakin and Parry, 2000) and raised questions about the citizenship status of this group of claimants. A senior official however saw the Chancellor's campaign as a positive step in promoting rights:

> "Winter fuel payments were a surprise, they were not part of the budgeting process. This was probably seeing the government at its most decisive and best, where they wanted to move very quickly ... quite a dramatic move ... the political sale is worth it."

However, another promotional innovation in June 2000 dented confidence in New Labour's expertise at 'good communication' and clearly was not seeing the government at its best. The 'NHS census' was portrayed as a unique chance for members of the public to comment on the NHS. There was little publicity to alert the public to the distribution of 12 million leaflets which, if they could be located, were to be returned within five days. The ineptitude of this exercise made it seem like a cheap publicity stunt rather than a serious attempt to find out what people's priorities were for modernising the health service.

An opportunity to test their public relations expertise arose when New Labour inherited the legacy of inaccurate information about the State Earnings Related Pension Scheme (SERPS), given to the public over many years. It was not an issue that could be ignored because the SERPS 'scandal', like other 'bad' news before, hit the media headlines, this time as "a story of injustice to individuals" (*Guardian*, 24 November 2000, p 1). It is detailed here at some length because it brings together many of the issues already encountered in this book.

Changes to pension policy by the Conservative government in 1986 meant that from April 2000 a husband or wife could inherit a maximum of one half of their spouse's SERPS entitlement. Until that time, they could inherit 100%. Correct details of the changes were published for about a year. In 1986, the Secretary of State "gave a commitment that there would be full publicity. For reasons which none of us understand nothing happened" (*Hansard*, 13 April 1999, col 615). From 1987 to 1996, information leaflets did not contain this change and, in addition, BA staff gave wrong information to people enquiring at local offices. Many were misled and lost out as a direct result (DSS, 2000d). It was to prove a costly mistake for the government.

Age Concern alerted the government to the issue in October 1998:

> People are shocked and angry to learn that if they lost their spouse on 6 April 2000 they will receive only half the SERPS payable had he or she died a day earlier.... As far as we know, there has been little general publicity and no attempt to inform individuals contributing to SERPS. We have also heard of a number of occasions where Benefits Agency staff have given incorrect information.... We are not surprised to learn of the ignorance that exists given the lack of publicity about this matter. (Age Concern, 1998b, p 1)

The DSS was faced with the task of sorting out the mess. One senior official commented:

> "We are struggling with that [SERPS] now. The advice in the last couple of weeks was the first we had heard about it ... leaflets should be automatically updated because it was a change in legislation.... Normally any leaflets we produce are developed in consultation with policy officials, so we don't know the details unless they tell us. So I can only imagine that something broke down."

An effective publicity campaign was necessary to make up for past mistakes. In a written answer to the House of Commons, the minister, Angela Eagle, said "We are actively looking at ways of raising public awareness of this change" (*Hansard*, 11 March 1999, col 344). By March 2000, the government described the failure as 'deplorable':

> The giving of wrong information by a government department is inexcusable. There is a clear responsibility to ensure that the information they provide is accurate and complete. In this case, it was not.... As a matter of principle we believe that when someone loses out because they were given the wrong information by a government they are entitled to redress. (DSS press release, 15 March 2000, 00/068)

An indication of how seriously the government took the affair can be gauged by the commissioning and publication of three separate reports. The recommendations were accepted and seem to be far-reaching for information providers. 'Root and branch' reforms of the DSS would include tightening up procedures for checking leaflets and guidance, external auditing of leaflets and other public information to ensure their accuracy and comprehensiveness, and ensuring that staff are kept up to date with changes in legislation.

The National Audit Office (NAO) report concluded that there had not been a deliberate attempt to misinform, but rather an administrative oversight, possibly the result of pressure of work at a time of resource shortage. The NAO saw a need for a change in the 'culture' of the DSS, "with assumptions in favour of more, rather than less, information being made available to the public" (NAO, 2000, p 3) and for enhanced accountability for information. It commented that "It is unlikely that the detailed content of leaflets was of concern very high up the organisation" (NAO, 2000, p 3). However, this explanation does not account for the fact that the leaflets *were* correct for the first year after the change had been announced.

Some people were more sceptical than the NAO. Baroness Castle of Blackburn, for example, thought that "The government were not anxious to publicise the change of what had been Labour's traditional policy" (*Hansard*, 13 July 1999, col 186). Others saw it as deliberate misinformation:

> More than misleading. A web of deceit on pensions. (*Guardian*, 18 August 2000, p 19)

There is conflicting evidence about the reasons for SERPS misinformation, but both Conservatives (in government at the time of the change) and New Labour accepted responsibility for poor administration. As a result, the proposed changes to the scheme were postponed. The onus – for this benefit only – was not on claimants to prove they had been misinformed in order to receive compensation. In addition to a publicity campaign in 1999/2000 costing £285,000 (DSS, 2000c, figure 9), the government is liable for a compensation package for this "series of colossal blunders" (*Hansard*, 29 November 2000, col 968) expected to cost £12 billion over 50 years. The costly nature of such poor administration is evident when this figure is seen in the context of the annual total social security budget of £95.6 billion in 1998/99 (DSS, 2000b, p 5) and annual expenditure on information (see Appendix A of this book). This unprecedented response to a failure to inform was a result of the vocal campaigning lobby of older people and those working with them. It provides a clear signal of the government's attitude to this group of citizens (discussed further in Chapter Eight of this book).

The resolution of the SERPS scandal placed a clear emphasis on rights. Other examples of information policy discussed earlier give mixed, ambivalent and sometimes contradictory messages about attitudes to citizenship. New Labour is explicit, however, in informing the public that rights are increasingly to be matched by responsibilities, in line with the Third Way redefinition of citizenship. Information policy to encourage people into work provides an example.

The government is continuing and developing a Thatcherite theme within the welfare benefit system, by "encouraging self-reliance, independence and the promotion of incentives to work" (Ditch, 1999, p 5). As New Labour tackles modernisation of the social security system, 'New ambitions for our country: A new contract for welfare' (Green Paper, 1998) pledges to "rebuild the welfare state around the work ethic: *work for those who can and security for those who cannot*" (emphasis in original). The attitude is clear: the message is tough and needs to be widely disseminated:

> The Prime Minister characterised worklessness as detachment from full citizenship. (Lister, 1998b, p 312)

There is to be no unconditional right to benefit for those deemed capable of work. The government is taking responsibility for improving citizens' chances of work through education and training. Help includes receiving information about benefit entitlements and a responsibility to take-up that assistance. It is an important strategic policy initiative for the government's overall economic and social agenda. The government recognises some of the problems:

> Many are missing out through ignorance. Sometimes they do not understand the system. But all too often the system has let them down before. Our plans will improve the level of service we provide – more readily available information through a personal adviser, more advice on potential eligibility to in-work benefits. (DfEE/DSS, 1998, p 11)

Generally, the introduction of personal advisers to provide information was welcomed, so long as sufficient resources were made available. There are fears, however, that benefits will be withdrawn from some individuals or groups, and uncertainty for lone parents who are unclear whether the interviews are compulsory (thus attaching conditions to benefit).

There were nevertheless positive reactions from officers in two voluntary agencies:

> "More recently there has been a shift again from a very remote service ... moving back to face-to-face interviews. I'm not sure that's about service to the customer but it's an interesting move back with an emphasis on personal advisers.... [It] may produce dividends: more accurate information from the start, more job satisfaction and more trust from claimants."

> "You make a claim for benefit and you would get a personal adviser, and I think part of the idea is that this person would have sufficient training to tell you not just about the benefit you originally went in to claim, but about all kinds of other things.... I have got lots of concerns about it, how much they

will do better off calculations, whether they would look at all the different scenarios, but potentially it's a positive step."

In the Standing Committee D Debate on the Bill (30 March 1999), Mr Rendel objected that this 'single gateway' was specifically and deliberately work-focussed. Targeting assistance and information at this group of claimants, rather than providing the scheme to those eligible for any benefits, fits with New Labour definitions of citizenship and with the way the social security system is developing. Dwyer (2000, p 95) comments that "certain social rights are increasingly conditional upon citizens first agreeing to conform to appropriate patterns of behaviour".

There has never been a statutory responsibility on the department to provide information or to increase benefit take-up levels. Administrative and financial objections to using information already held by DSS/BA or other government departments, which could make this possible, had been raised in earlier debates (Standing Committee B Debate on the Social Security Bill, 28 October 1997). Improving technology was already used to detect fraud. The minister, Keith Bradley, intimated in 1999 that in principle he was in favour of developing such a system, particularly for targeted groups. However, he explained that new integrated IT systems would be needed to take on this responsibility – and this would take time.

The Child Poverty Action Group (CPAG) rejected the reasons given by the minister: "Information about claimants is already used for purposes other than the benefit claim in question" (CPAG, 1998, p 6). Others were sceptical about government intentions. An officer of a voluntary agency expressed it this way:

> "The Minister says they want to be able to work towards that but they don't want it to become a statutory responsibility because that becomes very bureaucratic and you divert attention from what we can do to what we cannot meet. Also, they say it's unrealistic and there is not the IT at the moment. That may take a long time."

One politician agreed that it would take time but thought that a move was inevitable in the longer term, showing the way for more radical changes:

> "The need for ever more information is a symptom of the fact that the system is too complicated. The Benefits Agency have got no duty to do anything other than [answer questions] and that cannot be held against them. I think there are ways you could simplify it. After that you simply, at a stroke, statutorily impose a duty on the Benefits Agency to maximise people's benefits. Now if you did that you would impose a huge additional corpus of work on the BA and they will resist that furiously at the moment as things stand, but as the government goes further down the road of means-tested benefits I think that sooner or later that's almost inescapable. Actually, I believe that will be one of the drivers for simplification...."

In an encouraging move towards this goal, New Labour is exploring innovative ways of promoting welfare through e-government (Hudson, 2002; Margetts and Dunleavy, 2002). It has set the target that 100% of services should be online by 31 December 2005 (NAO, 2002). E-government offers the potential for a coherent information policy, for additional and effective ways of informing claimants about their entitlements, for claims to be made online and for more payments to be made automatically without the need for a claim (using data already held by government departments). The public can reasonably expect information provision to improve. Should it be successful, many of the difficulties of promoting welfare discussed in the book could be surmounted or reduced. It was recognised that, for example, better technology could have assisted the DSS in informing the public about changes to SERPS (NAO, 2002).

However, it should not be assumed that information and communications technology (ICT) will necessarily improve things. There are many hurdles to overcome. Some are to do with the supply side. Is the technology up to the job? Does ICT make the task of informing the public cheaper and more efficient? Can it replace the need for personal contact? How does ICT alter the relationship between government and its citizens? Are government departments and their staff willingly and enthusiastically supporting this approach? These are political, organisational and technological issues that are already familiar – before the concept of e-government – and discussed in earlier chapters of this book.

Other hurdles concern the demand side. Claimants with low levels of trust and low expectations, resulting perhaps from negative relationships with a government department, are unlikely to seek information in this way. Where earlier experiences of, or concerns about, new technology have not been good, there will be a reluctance to use ICT as a source. Unequal access to the Internet means that many who are eligible but are not claiming lack appropriate skills or are excluded from choosing these methods of finding out. To make use of e-government, claimants have to perceive the benefits of using electronic media over more traditional methods. Yet again these are familiar issues from earlier chapters of this book.

New Labour's targets go some way to acknowledging a right to information. ICT is contributing to public access to information and has the potential to increase the take-up of benefits. For the government's vision to be realised, there will need to be incentives for both information providers and citizens. It will require departments to be active in maximising the potential of ICT. There is, for example, the potential for diverse and non-discriminatory provision, rather than choices about *who* will be informed. Citizens will need to be active in using new technologies and take responsibility for finding out about their entitlements. However, new technology is not value-neutral and operates in the wider context of unequal power relationships. As with traditional methods of informing the public, the political context, culture and purpose of e-government will determine its success or failure.

In the meantime conflicting messages continue to complicate the picture for those wanting to understand New Labour policies and attitudes to rights and responsibilities. The conflicts are encapsulated in the following government rhetoric on information to the public. In a debate on welfare reform in the House of Commons, the Secretary of State, Alistair Darling, said:

> People will no longer ask of the system, 'What can you do for me?' They will ask, 'What can I do to help myself?'... If the government are to provide help, it is the responsibility of those seeking benefit or other support at least to find out what options are available. (*Hansard*, 28 October 1998, cols 340 and 354)

In contrast, in the same year the department's future aspirations were expressed thus:

> By 2020 our social security system will ... have staff clear about their role in delivering an Active Modern Service whereby: – those eligible for claiming benefits are sought out and told of their entitlement. (DSS, 1998d, p 53)

Summary

There has been a lot of information activity from New Labour, a government with a reputation for some expertise in 'spin'. Several reasons have been evident in this chapter. As a populist government it likes to spread 'good news' and to be seen to be 'doing something' (Hill, 1997). It uses publicity about welfare benefits as a way to educate the public and to distract attention away from 'bad news'. Information is also important to ensure the success of those social policies that are part of New Labour's wider social and economic agenda. However, there has been little publicity about New Labour's redistributive strategies. Fairclough (2000) sees this as a deliberate omission in order to retain middle-class electoral support.

This chapter has shown that the ambiguity of New Labour policies is reflected in its information provision for social security benefits. Policy making itself, of course, is the result of compromises; it is not a straightforward process. It involves making choices between complex demands, and often reconciling contradictions and tensions. The policies of previous administrations have also been shown to be contradictory or ambiguous in relation to information and rights. Under New Labour, there is continuity of information policy with previous administrations, and change and innovation. The clearest shifts in policy are demonstrated in attitudes to citizens as workers and to those citizens no longer expected to work. Information policy for these groups has been active and high profile. The case studies in Chapters Seven and Eight of this book analyse more detailed contemporary evidence.

However, ambiguity continues in attitudes and policies to other groups, for example disabled people and lone parents, and in activity to improve information to all claimants. Having said that, there is no ambiguity in the government's refusal to introduce a statutory duty to provide information about benefit entitlement to all those who are eligible but are not claiming. To do so would provide convincing evidence of a commitment to rights for all citizens.

SEVEN

Case study A: In-work benefits for low wage earners

This case study analyses government policies to provide information about social security benefits that are designed to supplement low wages, either for those already in work or that act as an incentive for the unemployed to take up employment. Having briefly described historical attempts to help those on low wages, this chapter explores chronologically the 'modern' benefits: Family Income Supplement (FIS), Family Credit (FC), and Working Families Tax Credit (WFTC). The link is also made to statistical evidence of rates of take-up (where figures are available) as a way of measuring the 'success' of the information policies themselves.

In-work benefits were chosen as a case study for several reasons. They were first introduced as part of the modern social security system in 1971, with different objectives to existing benefits. They have always been part of a wider agenda of social and economic policies, and the importance of their 'success' – that is, high levels of take-up by those entitled to claim – goes beyond the social security scheme itself. They reflect government values and moral agendas. Public and 'official' attitudes towards unemployed people in particular have been ambiguous and sometimes discriminatory, their 'citizenship' status being reflected in social security policy. In addition, effective information is particularly important for these means-tested payments that are based on complex qualifying conditions and complex calculations.

Wages and welfare

The problems of low wage earners were first recognised and acted upon at the end of the 18th century when, in 1795, magistrates at Speenhamland in Berkshire introduced a system of wage 'top-ups' to poor labourers. Until then, the Elizabethan Poor Law had assumed that people in work did not need assistance. This 'relief' was a response to rapid price inflation, with wages falling behind prices, and steep increases in the cost of living. To bring a man's earnings up to a minimum level on which he and his family could exist, amounts of 'relief' were linked to family size and to the price of bread. This practice spread nationwide and was enacted in an enabling amendment to the Poor Law on 24 December 1795 (de Schweinitz, 1961). The Speenhamland allowances were abolished in 1834 on the recommendation of the Royal Commission on the Poor Laws. The Commission was opposed to cash assistance for the working poor that could influence wage levels and encourage dependency on the state.

Those who needed assistance were deemed 'less eligible' than the poorest labourer and forfeited their citizenship.

Over half a century ago, Beveridge recognised the importance of supplementing low wages for families as an incentive to work. His report (Beveridge, 1942) presented to Parliament in December 1942 introduced a flat-rate Family Allowance for the second child and each subsequent child, partly as a response to this problem. It was assumed that one child could be supported adequately from family earnings. However, Family Allowance Rates did not increase in line with other benefits. By the late 1960s, there was evidence that a high proportion of low-income households consisted of families in full-time work (Stanton, 1977).

Family Income Supplement, 1971-88

Family Income Supplement (FIS) was a new kind of benefit, a 'novelty' (Stacpoole, 1972), with a new target group of claimants and a new type of administration. The Secretary of State for Social Services, Sir Keith Joseph, explained in his Second Reading of the Bill that FIS would be a more effective way to tackle family poverty, and was the first step in an overall campaign that aimed to help the poorest of the working population. FIS was replacing the Conservative government's pre-election pledge to increase a universal benefit with almost 100% take-up (Family Allowance), with a means-tested benefit which had to be claimed and would therefore rely on effective information for high levels of take-up (Atkinson, 1989). Although regarded as a stopgap measure until a more comprehensive tax/credit scheme was devised, informing those who were eligible and encouraging claims "was vital to its success" (*Hansard*, 10 November 1970, col 217). Barker (1971, p 75) questions how effective it would be:

> Will publicity be adequate? Will entitlement to FIS as a *right* be convincingly conveyed? (emphasis in original)

The 1970 Family Income Supplement Act made no mention of a duty to inform those who would be eligible.

The government's credibility was at stake in introducing this as a cheaper and, many thought, less effective way of tackling family poverty. Anticipating problems of take-up, questions were asked in the House of Commons about planned publicity several months before its introduction in August 1971 (claims could be made from May 1971). In December 1970, Sir Keith replied to a question in the House thus:

> I am planning an intensive publicity campaign beginning in the spring in which I shall seek the cooperation of social workers and others active in this field.... We are determined to do better in securing increased take-up than the previous Administration. (*Hansard*, 1 December 1970, col 1072)

Table 1: Government expenditure on Family Income Supplement publicity (1971-76)

Year	Expenditure (£)
1971	326,000
1972	309,000
1973	161,000
1974	124,000
1975	91,000
1976	172,000

Source: Hansard (6 December 1976, col 79)

An official in the Department of Health and Social Security (DHSS) at the time described the methods used as 'innovative' (Stacpoole, 1972). The government's efforts did not go unnoticed. For example, Hill (1976, p 67) comments that "This was an advance on some of the more half-hearted efforts made in the past". Table 1 shows that the minister's direct involvement and explicit determination to succeed resulted in expensive publicity campaigns (see also Appendix A of this book to put these figures into context).

However, from the start there were problems of low take-up with FIS and questions were asked again in the House of Commons. Sir Keith was asked about the 'failure' of the policy and why publicity was not successful:

> Will the right hon. Gentleman confirm that, despite a massive advertising campaign costing more than one third of a million pounds, the total take-up of this benefit, with only three weeks to go to the first day of receipt, is still only 10 per cent of those eligible, which is ridiculously far short of the right hon. Gentleman's declared objective of 85 per cent? (*Hansard*, 13 July 1971, col 192)

Estimates of take-up were to prove contentious from this time on, and an issue upon which there was both disagreement and a genuine difficulty in producing figures.

Although most commentators applauded the government's efforts to publicise FIS, take-up rates remained low. Blame was attached to the information provided to the public and to the complexity of FIS qualifying conditions and claim forms:

> One could be forgiven for thinking that the Government is conducting an advertising campaign for Balliol graduates, rather than those who had least educational resources spent on them. (Bottomley, 1972, p 12)

Hill (1990, p 95) agrees that information was not reaching its target:

> Family income supplement, introduced in the early 1970s, always had a comparatively low take-up. As a benefit going to the earning poor, its qualification conditions were particularly obscure and individuals were unlikely to be aware of their entitlement. (Hill, 1990, p 95)

The department was aware of the problems:

> We must assume that there are still many families who could claim but have not yet done so.... The practical question is, therefore, what can we do to find them and persuade them to claim.... We obviously need new techniques to find them. (Stacpoole, 1972, p 65)

The first leaflet (FIS 1, May 1971), was entitled 'Family Income Supplement: for families with children' (see Appendix B). Its rather drab design, flimsy paper and brief matter-of-fact detail is reminiscent of the tradition and style of official postwar leaflets, neither designed to inspire interest in the benefit nor to encourage claims. New techniques were found: "The advertising boys had been paid a record £61,000 in fees and Marjorie Proops had lent her talents to the campaign" (Field, 1973, p 3). The resulting poster featuring Proops is eye-catching and encouraging: "Thousands are benefiting from FIS. How about you? You could have a right to FIS of up to £4 a week" (FI 2, 1971).

The DHSS also appointed twelve 'FIS salesmen' for six months to provide information to professionals and potential claimants and to find out what was deterring claims. Lynes (1972, p 505) comments on this move:

> It is significant that the FIS salesmen are limiting their propaganda to the one benefit ... the decision to concentrate exclusively on FIS was partly political. For other benefits, the government can at least claim higher take-up rates than were reached under the Labour government. In the case of FIS, no such comforting comparison can be made. On the contrary, if FIS fails, the government can be blamed for introducing it in preference to higher family allowances.

The strategic importance of FIS to the government's wider agenda is confirmed by ministerial policies for selective information, high levels of resources and innovative activity.

Official estimates began to show an increase in take-up from 'about half' in 1972, to 'about two thirds' in 1973 and about 'three quarters' in 1974 and 1975 (Social Security Statistics). However, Field (1974, p 3) was sceptical:

> Despite a massive advertising campaign by the Government, which has already cost over £750,000 only about 50% of those families eligible claim the help to which they are entitled.

Campaigners began to conclude that low take-up was an inherent problem of means-tested benefits (CPAG, 1974).

The Supplementary Benefits Commission (SBC, 1975) had suggested that paid publicity is not necessarily the best way to get the message across. This view is confirmed by a statistical analysis of FIS recipients from 1971 to 1980 (Corden, 1995) and by Atkinson (1989, p 222), who concludes from his study over the same period that "there is no evidence that advertising campaigns have led to an appreciable increase".

Despite this, publicity continued and expenditure increased. At the time of the November 1979 uprating, an annual total of £294,000 was spent on advertising FIS on television and in the national press, and a total of £334,000 was budgeted for 1980, excluding leaflets (*Hansard*, 11 July 1980, col 343). Putting this into context, in 1980 £176,446 was spent in publicising free prescriptions and dental charges, and at least £1,000,000 in encouraging 'citizens' to exercise their right to buy council houses (Lorant, 1980). This was the first year of Thatcher's Conservative government, and these figures provide a useful reminder of her priorities (see Chapter Five for more on this campaign).

Information policy for the new Conservative government explicitly targeted "particularly vulnerable groups" (*Hansard*, 10 November 1980, col 66), including low-income working families. There was clear evidence of a new approach. The FIS leaflets and posters for 1981 had a new distinctive, colourful and attractive look. The leaflet (FIS 1) was well set out, clear and encouraging, featuring a smiling family group and the caption "How to claim extra money if you're bringing up children on low earnings" (see Appendix B of this book).

Despite the new approach, official figures estimated that only about 50% of those eligible were claiming FIS between 1981 and 1987, a disappointing figure for a government which had been proactive in its information policy. Evidence that the Conservatives were prepared to commit substantial resources to inform the public is clear from the £1.6 million spent publicising FIS between 1979 and 1984. This was *twice* as much as was spent on Housing Benefit and *16* times more than on Supplementary Benefit (calculations based on figures from Bradshaw, 1985, p 108).

Family Income Supplement was never the success that the governments had expected. The DHSS commissioned research among unemployed people and found that "None of the families knew the exact details [of FIS] but most did have a general idea" (Millar et al, 1989, p 78). Other unpublished government research even concluded that unemployed people are often "wholly unaware of the value and even the existence of 'in-work' benefits" (Millar et al, 1989, p 80). Research highlighted the difficulty of providing effective information about a complex system, and, as discussed in Chapter Three, the need to take claiming behaviour into account in formulating information policy.

Why were governments so anxious to promote and achieve high take-up rates of FIS? It was introduced as a measure to reduce the incidence of family poverty, yet was a politically controversial benefit. It was criticised for being less effective than an increase in Family Allowance, for its potential effect on wage levels, and for encouraging dependence on benefits. The government needed it to succeed; therefore, it gave priority to publicity for this, rather than other benefits. FIS was also part of the larger debate about universal versus selective benefits (Lynes, 1972; Atkinson, 1989). It became symbolic of a particular political ideology favoured by the Conservatives that guided the principles of the social security system:

> If the take-up of FIS was much higher than it is, then there would certainly be less reason for maintaining a non means-tested system of child support. (Deacon and Bradshaw, 1983, p 125)

Failure to maximise the take-up of FIS made that policy shift less easy to justify.

Family Credit, 1988-1999

Family Credit (FC) replaced FIS in 1988. Like its predecessor, it was aimed at increasing the income of low-waged families, both employees and the self-employed. Claimants would be better-off working than out of work and totally dependent on benefits. The government hoped and expected that take-up would be higher than it had been for FIS. In line with the other changes resulting from the Fowler Review of social security, FC was designed to be a simpler benefit, with rules more in line with those of Income Support and Housing Benefit. It was planned as an integral part of the benefit system, unlike the ad hoc policy of the FIS. How far it met its objectives would again depend on the level of take-up (Corden, 1999). This, in turn, would rely heavily on an effective information provision.

Norman Fowler, Secretary of State for Social Services, set a target take-up level of 60% (Lynes, 1991). The government expected a 'future trend' for FC to reach more than twice the number of families who received FIS (DHSS, 1988, p 273). As one politician involved at the time put it:

> "[We] mounted a major effort to increase take-up of FC. FIS just never took off. FC was an attempt if you like, both to get a benefit that was more likely to be taken up and ... in policy terms ... to get people to see that work was a genuine alternative to staying on benefit and indeed to create a financial incentive."

A simpler scheme did not tempt the government to think there was any less need for publicity and information for potential claimants, or to reduce its acceptance of responsibility to provide it. The 1986 Social Security Act, which introduced the scheme, recognised the need to make information about FC available (albeit in a way unlikely to provide an effective means of informing potential claimants):

The Secretary of State shall make copies of schemes prescribed under subsection (1) (a) or (b) [Family Credit] above available for public inspection at local offices of the Department of Health and Social Security at all reasonable hours without payment. (1986 Social Security Act, part 11, section 20.2)

One senior official suggested reasons for the Conservative government actively publicising the benefit in a planned and thorough way from the start:

"Family credit was pushed hard, lots of publicity, because it was an in-work benefit and Ministers were very keen on it. It was the really big theme. It was attractive because it did not cost a lot, the total cost was relatively low compared to other benefits, and it was attractive politically because it reinforced work. It had low take-up to begin with, but it picked up."

Hill (1990) writes that the FC take-up campaign was a 'significant exception' to the government's rather poor record on benefit publicity as a whole.

Table 2 gives details of expenditure on publicising FC as part of the total Department of Social Security (DSS) budget. It shows the importance to the government of this benefit, and therefore, its attitude to this group of claimants.

Table 2: Family Credit publicity expenditure as a percentage of the total DSS budget for information, publicity and advertising (1988/89-97/98)

Year	Total budget (£ million)	FC expenditure (£ million)	%
1988/89	12.8	3.4	27
1989/90	13.9	8	58
1990/91	14.6	4	27
1991/92	18	2	11
1992/93	18	2	11
1993/94	10.5	2.6*	25
1994/95	14.9	1.7*	11
1995/96	18.5	3	16
		1.9*	10
1996/97	13.4	2.7	20
1997/98	8.2	2.6	31

Note: There are some discrepancies in the figures between different sources.

Sources: Departmental reports and **Hansard*

Such a large proportion of the total budget – up to 58% in 1989/90 – sends important messages about the strategic importance of the benefit to the whole social security system and to the government's overall political agenda and priorities. A senior official involved at that time commented:

> "In the late 1980s, government information campaigns concentrated on those benefits related to work such as family credit, in line with their goal to reinforce the ethos of work and purpose of benefits."

However, initial indications were that the publicity did not result in achieving Fowler's 60% goal:

> Early estimates of the *take-up* of the new Family Credit in 1988 put the rate of those claiming against those entitled at about 30 per cent. (Alcock, 1990, p 92)

Lynes (1991) estimated a take-up rate of 50%.

The Central Office of Information evaluated the 1989 FC campaign. It found an increased awareness and understanding of the benefit among claimants, but no firm evidence that the number of claims had increased (Corden, 1995, p 27). Lynes (1991, p 9) comments:

> If the DSS has failed to raise take-up to a more respectable level, it is not for want of trying. Family Credit has been the subject of a series of advertising campaigns *without precedent* in the history of social security in Britain, at a cost of some £15 million. (emphasis added)

The department's imaginative efforts continued. An innovative campaign in the early months of 1991, 'Find out what's due to you', had several strands: a glossy brochure for advisers and social workers to enlist their support in encouraging claims, new television advertising to motivate people to look at their Child Benefit books which gave details about rates of FC payments, and posters and leaflets (DSS, 1991b). The leaflet (FC10) dated August 1991 was an attractive, colourful pocket-sized card giving figures – 'role models' – for FC payments for different types of families. Its tone was encouraging: "Whether yours is a two-parent or a one-parent family, you could be getting extra money every week from FC. It is NOT a loan, you don't have to pay it back" (FC10). Lynes (1991, p 9) was hopeful about this new campaign:

> The latest campaign, launched in February, may prove more successful ... for once the improvement [in take-up] may outlast the television advertising.

However, there were still doubts about the effectiveness of advertising campaigns. A study of administrative records of Family Credit claims by Ashworth and Walker in 1992 found that new claims were more likely to come from existing applicants – that is, those who already had information about their entitlement (Corden, 1995, p 27). The DSS did not publish estimates, but by 1992 the take-up of FC was still thought to be only around 50% (*Adviser*, 1992).

———

There was a policy shift in the early 1990s to target information and publicity about FC to the unemployed. The purpose of the campaign was clearly spelt out in the House of Commons by the minister, Mr Birt:

> The latest take-up advertising campaign is aimed at the unemployed and informs them of their potential to receive family credit which can act as a real incentive to getting back to work. (*Hansard*, 5 July 1993, col 7)

This was evidently in line with the government's wider objectives and with reducing both social security expenditure and dependency on benefits. A senior official involved in the campaign regarded it as "Nicely conceived, it worked well. Policy [division of DSS] got excited about it".

According to the DSS, the campaign reached its 1993-94 targets. For the first time it published estimated take-up figures for FC. Caseload based take-up increased from 66% to 69% between 1991 and 1995, and the following year (1996/97) increased to 72% (DSS press release, 1 October 1998, 98/249). The FC telephone helpline had opened in 1993. The high demand for information was reflected in the 4.5 million calls it received in the year ending April 1998 (Social Security Committee, 1998, appendix 15). However, not everybody was convinced of success. An advertising agency, brought in by the government to publicise back-to-work benefits, found that:

> The unemployed haven't a clue about Family Credit.... Family Credit's market recognition is zero.... It's just an unexpected bonus for those who've already decided to work.... The DSS is mocked as the Department of Total Obscurity with good reason. (Toynbee, 1998, p 14)

New Labour came to power in 1997. Their rhetoric was of maximising take-up, of reducing poverty and combating social exclusion. The department acknowledged the limitations of publicity and the need for radical action. However, citing administrative and technological reasons, the government refused to accept an amendment to the 1997 Social Security Bill which would make it a requirement to inform those entitled to the benefit (House of Commons Standing Committee B, 28 October 1997, col 48).

Why were all governments so anxious to achieve high rates of take-up of FC? It was a benefit devised, implemented and promoted by Thatcher's Conservative government at a time of high unemployment. Corden (1999) describes it as a 'prime example' of a benefit with strategic or political importance. She explains an anti-welfare government actively attempting to inform claimants of their rights thus:

> Its apparent key importance in maintaining work incentives has led government to assume responsibility for major promotional activity and investigation of ways of encouraging applications. (Corden, 1999, p 134)

The reality for FC publicity was high levels of spending and innovative activity. In the same year that 58% of the social security publicity budget was spent on FC campaigns (1989/90), only 8.5% of all benefit expenditure was paid out in FC. In 1997/98, 31% of the publicity budget and 2.5% of benefit expenditure was spent on FC (DSS, 2000c, table B1). This indicates priorities and, by implication, attitudes to other benefits and other claimant groups.

Family Credit was important as part of the government's overall economic and social policy. The benefit fitted with the Conservative government's values of self-reliance. Attitudes to what it meant to be a 'citizen' were clear, emphasising the importance of paid work. It also fitted with their goals of reducing the role of, and expenditure on, social security. Increasing take-up levels of FC moves claimants off total dependence on benefits, and reduces the social security budget at the same time as increasing National Insurance and Income Tax revenues. The Conservative government could justify expensive information and publicity campaigns in a period of high unemployment by longer-term financial savings. Johnson (1990) has an additional explanation, reminiscent of the evidence for promoting FIS. He describes the promotion of FC as part of a wider agenda of reforms, a trend that included increased means testing and a possible end to universal child benefit. Bennett (1987, p 125) agrees:

> There is a shift in the centre of gravity of the benefits system away from benefits as of right towards benefits requiring a 'test of income' as Norman Fowler likes to call it.

A politician recollects the rival arguments for its active promotion thus:

> "FC was devised as a contribution to answering the problem of families with children being the most likely to find themselves in the position where it did not pay them to work.... I don't think it was seen as a cheap option, but as a practicable option where nothing else looked practicable.... Yes it was political, but ... not part of an attempt to drive people back into work ... a way of making work more attractive to people who might otherwise feel there was no point – which is not quite the same thing."

The government estimated the take-up rate for 1998/99, the final full year of FC, as 66% to 70%.

Working Families Tax Credit

Working Families Tax Credit (WFTC) was introduced in the 1999 Tax Credits Act and replaced FC in October that year. The legislation does not place a duty to inform potential claimants, nor does it make any reference to providing information. It was an early policy change for the New Labour government. The Chancellor of the Exchequer, Gordon Brown, outlined his plans in his

'Green Budget' of 25 November 1997, some six months after coming into office.

WFTC shares many of the objectives of FC. It is designed to increase work incentives, to underpin the rewards of work and to break away from a welfare dependency culture. While building on the successful elements of FC and with more generous rates of payment, there is one important difference: it is a tax credit administered by the Inland Revenue (IR), a department within the Treasury, and is not a social security benefit. It was to be replaced by a more comprehensive system of tax credits in April 2003. The Treasury assumed 'centre stage' in welfare reform and employment strategy, emphasising the fundamental importance of WFTC to the Chancellor's overall economic project. A 'well-placed policy expert' observes that "When it comes to welfare reform Gordon [Brown] is the dominant figure" (Elliot et al, 1997, p 11). Deakin and Parry (2000, p 132) agree that the association between the DSS and the Treasury – the "pre-eminent policy Ministry" – amounted "almost to a colonisation by the Treasury".

The Chancellor's press release emphasises the new approach as "a tax and benefit system that makes work pay" (Treasury press release, 27 November 1997, 8). The introduction of a minimum wage in 1997 had dampened some criticism of welfare benefits as state subsidies of low wages. The new approach was considered very significant with regard to how the government felt about providing assistance that was less politically pejorative than welfare. One senior official expressed it thus:

> "The link with the tax system and pay packet demonstrate the reward of work over welfare. It was felt that a tax credit, rather than a welfare benefit, should reduce stigma and encourage take-up."

It was thought to be important also in how potential claimants were expected to feel about claiming. There was an important new message to get over to the public: "It's all about attitudes ... [for claimants] to feel better about themselves" (Inland Revenue, 1999). The head of the government task force reviewing the tax and benefits system, Martin Taylor, confirmed that by making payments through the wage packet:

> The principal psychological assertion ... is that the association of this payment with work rather than with the Benefits Agency will change the way people think about it. I am just as attached to the idea that associating it with the fact of working is a positive change as that taking it away from the welfare system is the removal of a negative. (Social Security Committee, 1998, p xiii)

Crucial to the policy's success would be how publicity and information provision would be approached. The change to a tax credit had important administrative implications for the provision of information to the public. One senior official explained:

> "The culture of the Inland Revenue is different, the old Whitehall image, bowler hats and so on. This is not the reality but it's a stereotype which perhaps they play on, jokey about our attitudes to tax. Not many people warm to the Inland Revenue, but the way a benefit is promoted makes a huge difference."

The IR was accustomed to collecting not offering money and to providing information to groups other than benefit claimants. One local authority welfare rights worker thought this was a disadvantage:

> "The IR is not as customer focussed [even] as the BA. It's not used to dealing with this particular client group ... but there will be [some] continuity of staff. They need to be very careful. Working Families Tax Credit is the big one. It has to succeed."

The importance of improving take-up rates by effective publicity was recognised by the responsible minister, the Paymaster General, Dawn Primarolo: "Take-up is clearly linked to eligibility and information" (*Hansard*, 26 January 1999, col 156). The IR was optimistic, particularly following their recent success with 'Hector', the income tax self-assessment campaigns. One senior official commented:

> "This was a new group of people for the Revenue to interact with. Would that fact ... make this a problem? So we did a lot of research to try and explore that.... I think it was honestly the first time that government had gone out with such an overt message to say 'This is money you are entitled to, this means more money'.... I felt that this was something where people were actually prepared to trust us in terms of the information.... For the first time we have launched a campaign that offered people money."

The Chancellor's first full budget on 17 March 1998 promised that WFTC would be more generous than FC, "Because in future work will pay, those with an offer of work can have no excuse for staying at home on benefits". The moral themes are reminiscent of Sir Keith's aspirations for FIS in 1971:

> The 1998 Budget embodied a serious shift of resources into families with children, especially working families, costing over £2.5 billion a year when fully implemented.... Brown's aim is still to secure a new paradigm of welfare based on a self-reliant ethical socialism in a society nourished by the notion of inclusion through hard work. (Deakin and Parry, 1998, p 52)

Definitions of citizenship became more explicitly linked to responsibilities and to paid work in particular. The theme, 'Work is the best form of welfare', was constantly repeated by the new government in their efforts to get the message across. The themes of opportunity, poverty and helping people into jobs recurred in press releases and reports in the run-up to the introduction of WFTC. The link between social security and labour market policies reinforced the importance of effective publicity to the overall success of the Chancellor's wider project. Requiring unemployed people to attend an interview to discuss their options for work would, inter alia, provide an opportunity of informing people of their rights to the tax credit.

In the months before WFTC was introduced, staff were concerned about how publicity would affect workload. A successful publicity campaign would result in an estimated 400,000 additional families claiming WFTC from October 1999. Staff concerns were met with reassurance that advertisements would be sufficiently clear to deter claims from those not eligible (Inland Revenue, 1999). Concern was also expressed by the Social Security Committee (SSC) about administrative readiness and whether the IR could cope. The IR devised a strategy of targeting families who were likely to be eligible, and of drawing on the experience of the existing FC unit (Social Security Committee, 1998). However,

> The Committee is not wholly satisfied by these reassurances. Our Report on the introduction of Disability Living Allowance and Disability Working Allowance in 1993 gives a dreadful warning of the debacle which can occur when officials underestimate the surge in demand when a new benefit is introduced. (Social Security Committee, 1998, p x)

That 'debacle', discussed earlier in this book, had caused distress to claimants and resulted in long delays in processing claims. The issue of balancing the need to encourage take-up with the need not to overwhelm the administration was familiar to information policy makers.

The SSC's concern about administrative readiness did not distract it from the importance of encouraging claims. The IR's assurance that it accepted the onus of responsibility for achieving maximum take-up of WFTC and Disabled Persons Tax Credit (DPTC) still did not satisfy the committee, which had more radical suggestions. Suspecting that statutory responsibilities to deliver the tax credit would take precedence over other (discretionary) activities such as publicity, the Committee

> recommend that a *duty* be placed on the Inland Revenue to take all reasonable steps to ensure that people who are eligible to claim WFTC and DPTC (including the child care tax credit) are made aware of their entitlement and encouraged to claim.... Much more needs to be done if WFTC is to fulfil its potential in guaranteeing all working families a decent minimum income. (Social Security Committee, 1998, p xvi; emphasis added)

The Social Security Committee further recommended that the government consider the use of 'data matching' between government departments to identify eligible families.

The Chancellor responded to these suggestions in a letter to the Chairman of the Committee, dated 22 January 1999. His commitment was important to the campaign, but fell short of the Committee's recommendations:

> Encouraging all those eligible for the new tax credits to apply for them will be an important objective for the Inland Revenue and they will be undertaking a wide-ranging publicity campaign. Existing data will be used at every opportunity ... to help identify potential applicants and focus the advertising and information campaign on the most appropriate people. The Revenue will commission tracking research to monitor the effectiveness of its publicity and information campaigns.... Information and advice will continue to be available to potential applicants as part of the normal service supplied by the Benefits Agency and Employment Service.... The dedicated helpline currently giving a majority of the detailed advice on Family Credit and Disability Working Allowance will be transferred to the Inland Revenue. (Social Security Committee, 1999, p v)

A Treasury press release (22 June 1999, 102/99) gave initial details of the publicity campaign, which was launched by the Chancellor at 11 Downing Street on 7 September 1999. The Prime Minister appeared with Brown on breakfast television, reinforcing the importance not only of the policy itself but also the high profile information campaign. The campaign for this 'flagship policy' had priority and a large budget because it was the Chancellor's initiative. The political importance of WFTC was widely understood. Politicians, for example, commented:

> "They were looking for a political splash, and with the Chancellor driving it there was not going to be any shortage of money because he was signing the cheques.... If Gordon Brown is still at the Treasury [in five years] he will make it work and he will spend whatever it takes to make it work."

> "The decision about the £12 million is the Chancellor's. It's obviously a high priority for the government, it's the lynchpin of the 'making work pay' bit of the equation, and therefore it was always going to be important. It's fairly obvious to predict that we'd want to spend some money on it. It's important that people know what their entitlements are."

The publicity budget for the campaign – £12 million – was more than the combined budgets of the DSS and the BA in 1997/98 – £8.2 million – which was to promote *all* benefits (see Appendix A of this book).

There were several strands to the campaign – television, press, regional ministerial conferences, posters and leaflets – which set out to be both informative and entertaining (see leaflet WFTC/BK 1, in Appendix B of this book). The emphasis of the campaign was not only on rights to claim but also on the moral agenda. In offering an alternative to dependence on benefits, certain behaviour was expected, giving clear messages about what it is to be a citizen. One politician commented:

> "If you look at the introduction of WFTC, that's very much about trying to say to people 'Look this is the deal, really. You should work and we're going to help you try to get jobs. It might take training but here's the bargain. If you do that we'll help you with child care costs and we'll make sure work pays with the WFTC'."

A Treasury press release on 5 October 1999 (162/99) announced that the WFTC campaign "has resulted in the biggest response to a Government advertising campaign ever, with almost 350,000 enquiries from the public". By 31 May 2000 there were 1,061,000 current awards, 76% of the target group (Inland Revenue, 2000). Launching a £5 million advertising campaign in October 2000, a year after WFTC was introduced, the Chancellor announced that 300,000 more families were claiming WFTC than FC at its peak (Treasury press release, 23 October 2000, 116/00). The government later published the first estimated take-up rate for WFTC. In 2000/01 this was a disappointing 62-65%, lower than the rate for the final year of FC.

Why is New Labour so keen to maximise the take-up of WFTC and devote unprecedented resources to providing information to the public? The WFTC is a New Labour policy announced within months of their election victory. The values underlying it perpetuate and extend the previous Conservative administration's policies. Paid work – not dependency on benefits – is to be 'the best form of welfare' and carry with it the status of citizenship. The change from a welfare benefit to a tax credit and the Chancellor's personal promotion of WFTC demonstrate its importance to his economic and social justice agendas. Areas of concern were about administrative readiness and the way it would be paid – the ongoing debate since the 1980s about benefits paid through 'the wallet or the purse' – rather than the opposing principles of universality and means testing as a way of reducing poverty.

The new government's need to be seen to be making a difference also helps to underline the importance of this high level campaign. The Chair of the Social Security Committee, Archy Kirkwood, commented on the speed of implementation of WFTC:

> I perfectly understand that there is a political agenda and that the Government want to get the scheme up and running for the next election so that they can put it in the shop window. (*Hansard*, 26 January 1999, col 189)

Reducing poverty is one measure on which the Prime Minister is prepared to be tested by the electorate. WFTC is a part of the agenda "of ending child poverty in a generation" (Brown, 1999, p 19), and part of redefining what it means to be a citizen. One politician described it this way:

> "It is not cynical to say that it was an entirely politically driven agenda that set all of that [WFTC] campaign up, because if it had been otherwise there would have been campaigns in the past which would have advertised other benefits in a way that would have increased take-up considerably."

Summary

Family Income Supplement was introduced in 1971 by a Conservative government forthright about their determination to tackle family poverty. The 'rediscovery of poverty' in the 1960s impelled action. It was a controversial policy and a cheaper alternative to increasing Family Allowances. It was also part of the Conservative's longer-term aim for social security, that of shifting from universal to selective benefits. If the expected level of take-up could be achieved at a time of high employment – unemployment stood at 3.5% in 1971 (*Social Trends*, 1976) – this policy could be seen to be making a difference. Planned, targeted and well-resourced information policies for FIS contrasted with negative attitudes towards the citizenship status of unemployed people. The priority given to FIS campaigns illustrates the degree to which success was important to the government's credibility and image, and strongly supports 'political' arguments for information policy. However, despite high levels of activity and expenditure governments failed to overcome the apparently inherent problems of informing many of those who were eligible. The complex scheme never achieved hoped-for levels of take-up.

In 1988, the Conservatives introduced FC as a simpler scheme and part of a strategy to maintain work incentives. Unemployment had been rising steadily since the late 1970s, peaking in 1986 at 11.2% (*Social Trends*, 1991) when the legislation to introduce FC was enacted. This may explain why an apparently anti-welfare government gave priority to an active and innovative benefit information campaign. Promoting FC was expected to further their overall economic and moral agenda, reducing the social security budget while reinforcing the value of work and self-reliance. A commitment to inform was not constrained by resources – as much as 58% of the total social security publicity budget was spent on promoting in-work benefits in one year. Success would also vindicate a shift away from universal welfare benefits. There was an increase in take-up, but not to expected levels. As with FIS, the evidence points to overriding 'political' arguments for information provision, in particular the values and goals of Thatcher's government.

Working Families Tax Credit was introduced in 1999 by the New Labour government. This is an explicitly welfare-to-work government, whose policies increasingly match opportunities with responsibilities in line with New Labour rhetoric and values. The new approach is reflected in the transfer of the 'benefit' to the IR as part of a policy to integrate the tax and benefit systems. It is no longer to be regarded as a welfare benefit. WFTC is the incentive for 'making work pay'. Increasingly, citizenship has become redefined around work and New Labour's social security policies are "premised on paid work obligations" (Lister, 1998b, p 325). Unprecedented resources have been devoted to overcoming what had previously seemed to be inherent difficulties in informing the public. Take-up rates for WFTC are disappointingly low, and policies fall short of imposing a duty to inform. The strategic importance of WFTC to a wider political and economic agenda is clear from the Treasury's pivotal role and the Chancellor's own active involvement in its promotion. Thus, 'political' influences are again strongly evident in information policy. New Labour's need to be seen to make a difference and a commitment to reduce family poverty is also evident in information policy, reinforced by historical reasons for the sensitivity of the policy issue itself.

Since 1971, governments have made exceptional efforts to promote in-work benefits at the expense of welfare benefits for other claimant groups. There is a marked shift here from neoliberal attempts to reduce benefit dependency, with the implications discussed in earlier chapters of this book for definitions of citizenship and for information policy. Information policy aiming to encourage people to claim their 'right' to FIS in the early 1970s has increasingly become information to enable citizens to fulfil their responsibility to work. The corollary is that citizens have a responsibility to claim their 'right' to WFTC and there is no stigma in doing so. Citizenship, for 'those who can', is about work and about claiming those benefits that make work an attractive option.

EIGHT

Case study B: Means-tested benefits for older people

This case study analyses government policies to inform older people of their rights to means-tested benefits. It begins by briefly describing the social security benefits designed for older people and the demographic and financial situation of older people in the UK. These data put the case study into context and explain the importance of benefit schemes for both government and for older people themselves. The chapter then takes a brief historic view of central government policies on information about means-tested financial assistance for older people; that is, National Assistance, Supplementary Benefit and Income Support. The main focus of the chapter is the New Labour government's information policy for Income Support/Minimum Income Guarantee.

This case study was chosen to illustrate the link between providing information and attitudes to citizenship. There has been a long-standing recognition of under-claiming by older people and of a link between older age and poverty. However, it was New Labour's explicit commitment to older people, especially those living in poverty, which resulted in April 1998 in a radical pilot scheme to find ways of informing this group of their eligibility for Income Support. The case study explores why concern about older people as a group resulted at this time in more active and targeted information.

The citizenship status of older people is ambiguous. Seen as 'deserving' in some ways, older people are also characterised by negative images based on the devalued status accorded to unproductive older people in western, capitalist societies (Phillipson, 1981). Walker (1998, p 249) observes that "Britain is a country in which age discrimination, or ageism, is widespread". Ageism influences – and is perpetuated by – policies on health, housing, employment, personal social services and social security. Health policy, for example, denies some older people treatment purely on the basis of their age. Epstein (quoted in Tinker et al, 1993, p 13) found "disheartening evidence that these workers [health staff] may be neither equipped nor *inclined* to provide information to elderly people" (emphasis added).

The previous chapter concluded that information policies for unemployed people and low wage earners, despite their sometimes ambiguous citizenship status, were generally and perhaps surprisingly research based and clear in their objectives. This case study will enable comparisons to be made with information policy for another group of citizens.

Older people and benefits in the UK

The chapters of this book so far have shown that the complexity of the social security system is a problem for both would-be providers of information and for those eligible to claim. Benefits for older people are no exception. Some benefits are designed for all people aged 60+ (for example, winter fuel payment is paid automatically to all who are eligible). Some are paid to those who have sufficient national insurance contributions and are over retirement age (for example, retirement pension, which has to be claimed but has almost 100% take-up). Other benefits have their own particular eligibility conditions. Those which are the subject of this case study have both capital and income limits. As means-tested benefits they have to be claimed and therefore known about. Information is the key.

It is important for this study to be aware of the impact of older people on government policies. In 2000, 15.6% of the population of the UK were aged 65+. In 1998/99, 48% of social security benefit expenditure was paid to older people (*Social Trends*, 2002). Older people form one of the largest groups living in poverty in the UK. One third of older people (3.3 million) live in poverty (as defined by living below 50% of average income after housing costs) (Walker, 1998, p 253). The association between low income and old age too often results in exclusion (Age Concern, 1998a; DSS, 2000b). Definitions of poverty and its relationship to levels of means-tested benefits have been extensively discussed since 1948 (see, for example, Atkinson, 1969; Townsend, 1979; Spicker, 1993). This case study is not a contribution to that debate. However, failure to claim entitlements can only exacerbate the incidence and degree of poverty.

On its own, the basic Retirement Pension fails to provide adequate income. This is officially acknowledged by comparing the single person rate of Retirement Pension (£77.45) with the 'safety net' or 'top up' rate of Income Support (£102.10) – known as Minimum Income Guarantee (MIG) for claimants aged 60+ (rates from April 2003). Since the introduction in 1980 of the present policy of increasing Retirement Pensions in line with prices and not earnings (Alcock, 1990), an increasing number of older people have been eligible for means-tested benefits. However, evidence shows that older people are among the least likely to apply for benefits where there is a means test (Johnson and Falkingham, 1992). Those who do not apply for the benefits to which they are entitled fail to bring their income up to that minimum level.

Lack of information has always been a key reason why older people do not claim (Townsend, 1979; Kerr, 1982; Age Concern, 1998a). An evaluation of a Greater London Council benefits take-up campaign found that older people had the lowest information levels of any claimant group before the campaign, and that, even after the campaign, their awareness of where to seek advice was still substantially lower (Victor, 1986). A National Customer Survey in the 1990s found that pensioners were still the least well informed group among those who were in touch with the Department of Social Security and/or the Benefits Agency (Cummins, 1996, p 98). Of the many variables which influence take-up among older people who are eligible but not claiming, the role of information is too often treated only peripherally (Silverstein, 1984).

Information for older people (1948-97)

This section briefly explores government information policies about means-tested financial assistance for older people from 1948 until 1997. It is divided into three parts, looking in turn at National Assistance, Supplementary Benefit and Income Support to prepare the ground for a more detailed examination of New Labour's policies to inform older people of their entitlements.

National Assistance (1948-66)

The scene was set for the introduction of National Assistance by a special Assistance Board enquiry in 1947 into the financial position of pensioners. The 1948 National Assistance Act conferred a 'duty' on the Board "to assist persons in Great Britain who are without resources to meet their requirements" (section 4.4). The 1949 Report of the National Assistance Board (NAB), while acknowledging the necessity of information and publicity for those eligible, expressed the hope that very few people "in need of the Board's help are going without it" (NAB, 1949, p 18). As discussed in Chapter Four, it seemed clear to policy makers that the problems associated with the Poor Law, particularly low take-up, had been overcome (Deacon, 1982).

Despite the optimism, by the mid-1950s there was plenty of evidence to show that all was not well, particularly for pensioners:

> Assistance was under-utilised ... for a mixture of reasons such as ignorance of the benefits available.... It is important to remember that a substantial proportion of the elderly poor were probably failing to apply for national assistance from the earliest years of its existence. (Webb, 1975, p 428)

Many official reports and academic studies confirm that significant numbers of older people were not claiming their entitlements (see Phillips Committee, 1954; Cole and Utting, 1962; Townsend, 1963; Abel-Smith and Townsend, 1965; Allen Committee, 1965; Townsend and Wedderburn, 1965). Townsend (1979) estimates that three quarters of those interviewed in his survey during the 1950s and 1960s were unaware of their eligibility because of the lack of effective publicity. The research findings had an impact. The Labour opposition called it a 'national disgrace' and came up with a policy for an income guarantee to replace National Assistance. In 1964 the Conservative government proposed an enquiry into the causes of non-take-up. The issue had become party political and required action. Webb (1975, p 428) comments that "pensioner poverty was a potential electoral embarrassment". Pressure began to mount for a reform of National Assistance (Cole and Utting, 1962).

How did the NAB approach the problem of under-claiming and ignorance?

> Changes had begun to occur in national assistance during the early 1960s.
> In particular the amount of publicity given to benefits had been increased
> even before 1964. (Webb, 1975, p 454)

The Labour Party's plans in opposition for social security and older people
were gaining them credibility. The issue was one of Prime Minister Wilson's
personal priorities before the 1964 election (Webb, 1975). Evidence presented
in previous chapters of this book has shown that such high level commitment
is critical to policy success. Webb (1975, p 453) observes that "The elderly
were the largest and the only socially approved group of nationally assisted
applicants", confirming their citizenship status at that time.

The minister, Richard Wood, expressed the wish to find positive ways of
encouraging claims:

> I believe that the best approach to this problem ... is to try to take positive
> steps to spread more widely information about the services which the Board
> is prepared to offer.... I have recently taken the positive step of putting a
> new leaflet in every pensions book which has the object of trying to ease
> the way for people into National Assistance. (*Hansard*, 22 June 1964, col
> 16l)

The new explanatory leaflet, entitled 'Twenty questions' (NAB, AL 51, nd; see
Appendix B of this book), produced in 1964, was printed on flimsy paper in
orange, black and white. It was factual and reassuring rather than encouraging,
but it did stress that the benefit was a 'right'. While conceding the difficulty of
gauging the precise effect of publicity, a survey carried out just before and just
after the leaflet was issued concludes that the package of special publicity
measures had been effective in making up the minds of "some thousands of
elderly people" to make a claim (NAB, 1965).

The government's concern also led the Ministry of Pensions and National
Insurance (MPNI) to hold an enquiry in 1965: *Financial and other circumstances
of Retirement Pensioners* (MPNI, 1966). The enquiry set out to find out how
many pensioners were living in poverty and the barriers which prevented them
from claiming. It found that 850,000 (16%) retirement pensioners were entitled
to National Assistance but were not receiving it. The most frequent reason for
not claiming, for more than a third of those questioned, was a lack of information
or misconceptions about eligibility. It "points to a need for more extensive
advertising of the available provisions" (Atkinson, 1969, p 58), and for information
that was accessible and accurate. However, there was by this time more
fundamental dissatisfaction with the scheme and growing pressure for reform
(Hall et al, 1975; Deacon, 1982).

Supplementary Benefit (1966-88)

The 1966 Ministry of Social Security Act replaced National Assistance with Supplementary Benefit. Although there was still no statutory duty to inform, the government's information policy was planned, active and coherent. Pensioner poverty had become a politically sensitive issue. The Labour government had staked their credibility on action to relieve the poverty of 'deserving' pensioners. Prime Minister Wilson had made a personal commitment to older people before the election.

In an attempt to overcome the barrier of ignorance and to encourage claims, the ministry "embarked on an extensive advertising campaign, boosting Supplementary Benefits as 'Social Security's Best Buy'" (Atkinson, 1969, p 62). Bull (1970, p 8) comments on the new approach:

> The Labour government's publicity for welfare benefits at first appears encouraging. Its Ministry of Social Security Act of 1966 marked a new emphasis on the 'right' to a means-tested benefit, and £48,220 was spent on advertising this new deal for pensioners.

It was noticeable that, compared to National Assistance, the design and language of leaflets and posters was attractive, clear and encouraging to potential claimants (for example, DHSS SB29, nd; see Appendix B of this book).

However, the government's initial enthusiasm for providing information and publicity for Supplementary Benefit did not last. This may in part be explained by the economic crisis of the 1970s and limited scope for welfare reform. It may have been compounded by public and media hostility towards the social security system, and towards claimants in general (Walker, 1982). Increasingly, there was also the feeling that "there is something inherent in benefits designed for the poor which makes for poor publicity and poor administration" (CPAG, 1968b, p 3).

Under-claiming remained stubbornly at previous levels. The Child Poverty Action Group (CPAG) reported that "possibly as many as one million old people are eligible for, but do not claim, supplementary benefit" (CPAG, 1974, p 3). By 1979, official estimates indicated that 35% of pensioners were not receiving the Supplementary Benefits to which they were entitled (*Hansard*, 5 April 1982, col 248). The 1980 Social Security Act aimed again at simplification and a clearer understanding of the scheme for both claimants and staff (DHSS, 1978; Walker, 1982) but by 1986 the take-up rate for pensioners was still only 67% (Social Security Statistics).

Income Support from 1988

Income Support replaced Supplementary Benefit in 1988. Government rhetoric again expressed a commitment to information and to rights, but the 1986 Social Security Act fell short of placing a duty on the department to inform potential claimants. Key themes for the Conservative government at this time, as discussed earlier, were reducing expenditure, simplifying administration, targeting of benefits and reducing dependency. These themes are clearly at odds with maximising take-up of benefits by older people (and others). It was by now generally accepted that one million pensioners entitled to Income Support were not claiming (Age Concern, 1998a; Walker, 1999).

Leaflets and posters improved in design, clarity and attractiveness, but evidence has shown that there had been an improvement in information about *all* benefits at this time (despite a government committed to reducing expenditure and dependence on benefits). Routine information provision was supplemented by ad hoc publicity initiatives. For example, there was a take-up exercise in 1989 to accompany the introduction of enhanced pension premiums. These were an addition to Income Support for claimants aged 75-79. However, the campaign was not a success. One senior official involved at the time remembered that the experience deterred information policy makers from mounting future campaigns:

> "Unfortunately we can't locate the papers, they have been destroyed, not for any malicious reasons, there was no evaluation done. We know there was a national campaign but unfortunately the collective memory here in DSS HQ was ... that it went terribly badly because all it did was to raise expectations among an enormous amount of pensioners who were not entitled to enhanced pensioner premium.... There was a lot of criticism of the department afterwards ... that was introduced under a Conservative administration and there was a genuine feeling among Ministers that really this could be a device that did not work particularly well."

Targeting information in this way had already provoked criticism in the House of Commons, raising questions about the status of different groups of claimants:

> One section of the population that is in need, about which the government is concerned, is the elderly – purely because of their numbers, one suspects. They have employed those methods to ensure that some elderly people get more benefit, but as soon as it is lone parents, the unemployed, or single unemployed persons claiming benefit, the Government strongly object. But they all have rights under the legislation. (*Hansard*, 23 July 1986, col 445)

The question of low take-up among older people did not go away. Age Concern (1998a) estimated a take-up rate of between 60% and 66% in 1995/96. The figure of one million pensioners not claiming the Income Support to which they were entitled was brought to public attention by government information campaigns and media coverage of the change to automatic payment of Social Fund cold weather payments in 1991. Those who were eligible for but not receiving Income Support would not receive that payment either. Low take-up became a party political issue. In the run-up to the 1997 General Election, the Labour party, as in the early 1960s, made commitments to tackle the problem.

Summary

The estimated level of under-claiming by older people remained remarkably consistent for the first five decades of the welfare state. The rhetoric throughout the period is of rights to benefit and commitments to inform claimants. The reality is of mostly sporadic activity, rather than planned and coherent policies, to publicise and provide information to older people about National Assistance, Supplementary Benefit and Income Support. Activity increased and improved after changes to the system, but despite some high level commitment to the issue, information policy was never as effective in increasing take-up as promised and expected.

> For more than half a century, governments have been concerned about low take-up of means-tested benefits by older people and have sought, with limited success, to improve the situation by publicity campaigns and periodic changes of name. (NPC, 1999, p 5)

'New Labour' and information for older people

The New Labour government's pre-election manifesto promises:

> We will examine means of delivering more automatic help to the poorest pensioners – one million of whom do not even receive the Income Support which is their present entitlement. (Labour Party, 1997a, p 27)

Previous administrations had made similar promises, but had not succeeded. New Labour's radical approach in 1997 was different, but how far was it a genuine desire to see older people receive their rights as citizens?

Background

While Labour was in opposition, two important documents were published that indicate that the issue would have priority if they came into office. The Report of the Commission on Social Justice (Borrie, 1994) recognises that there were 570,000 older people officially estimated as eligible for Income Support but not claiming. The Labour Party manifesto makes a commitment to pensioners sharing in the increasing prosperity of the nation. It criticises Conservative policies for pensioners which "have created real poverty, growing inequality and widespread insecurity" (Labour Party, 1997a, p 26).

A few weeks after the election, in response to a question about Benefits Agency targets to increase the level of take-up, Keith Bradley, Social Security Minister, explained in a written answer:

> Our priority is to get help to around one million pensioners not taking up their income support entitlement. We are determined to address this issue, and we are currently commissioning research to establish why they do not claim the benefit which is their due. (*Hansard*, 23 June 1997, col 417)

In a speech to the Labour Party Conference later that year, the Prime Minister, Tony Blair, was eloquent in his personal commitment to pensioners' welfare in a reformed welfare state:

> I don't want ... a country ... where people who fought to keep that country free are now faced every winter with the struggle for survival, skimping and saving, cold and alone, waiting for death to take them.... I will not rest until ... the old are cherished and valued to the end of their days.... Our number one duty is to get help to the poorest pensioners first. (Blair, 1997, p 11)

Motions to that same conference call for 'speedy' help to the one million pensioners not receiving the Income Support to which they are entitled, and urge the use of modern technology to identify them (Labour Party, 1997b).

There was also external pressure for action. The UN Committee on Economic, Social and Cultural Rights, in their five-yearly review of Britain's compliance with the 1967 International Covenant, reported that it was 'disturbed' that an estimated one million pensioners were not claiming the social security benefits to which they were entitled. It mentions "unacceptable" levels of poverty in Britain because of "self-imposed budgetary constraints" (*Guardian*, 10 December, 1997, p 1).

It was the Chancellor, Gordon Brown, in his 'green' or pre-budget statement, who announced that there would be pilot projects "to identify the best ways of providing more automatic help to the estimated one million pensioners not currently receiving the income support to which they are entitled" (Treasury press release, 25 November 1997, 5). The Treasury allocated £15 million to the projects (to include expenditure on the programme, as well as administration and evaluation), which were a direct response to New Labour's manifesto (Croden et al, 1999). In 1997, the DSS estimated that there were 1,010,000 pensioners entitled – but not claiming – Income Support (due to 'an error' there was a provisional revised estimate in December 1998 of between 400,000 and 700,000) (Croden et al, 1999, p 12).

The pilot scheme was generally welcomed, although cautiously by some. Alcock (1998, p 29) describes it as a "major departure from recent service delivery priorities, and is at last perhaps a recognition of the need for a welfare rights agenda within the benefits service". An officer in one voluntary agency described it as "an innovation" and "a huge concession" to admit that this number of pensioners were losing out. A senior ex-official in the department agreed that it demonstrated a radical shift in policy:

> "I think it must have changed now because of this thing about pensioners ... the Treasury were concerned in the past about the increase in expenditure."

Nor was its significance, and the high level of commitment, lost on current officials, one of whom commented:

> "The financing of take-up is unusual ... and in a broad way that's down to the Treasury, you don't have to bid for that money ... we are deliberately going out and finding out why they don't claim and encouraging them to do so.... Information provision is fundamental to the scheme working, plus the emphasis of the Prime Minister on the lot of the poorest pensioners in his conference speech and an emphasis which he has repeated since then. That's obviously something they are philosophically and politically deeply committed to."

Other observers were more sceptical about the government's motives. One voluntary agency worker commented, "One can be cynical and say they are getting all the kudos for targeting this group but actually not having to put out very much money", while another said, "It all counts for votes". Age Concern (2000, p 56) also expresses concern about how committed New Labour really is to relieving pensioner poverty. It suspects other agendas:

> Low take-up of benefits is widely perceived as an anachronism.... There is a lingering suspicion that governments welcome (and even perhaps rely on) low take-up to help balance the books.

Walker (1999, p 521) echoes previous doubts about the efficacy of means testing itself:

> As welcome and long overdue as these measures to increase take-up are, past experience does not justify the government's confidence in means testing. Successive governments have tried the same thing, with little success, which is why just under one million pensioners live below the income support poverty line. Providing advice is not enough.

The pilot project

The project started in April 1998 in nine selected areas and was scheduled to run for six months. It was based on previous take-up work by local authorities and other non-government organisations, and would give practical back-up to two ongoing research projects also due for completion in October 1998. These research projects (Costigan et al, 1999; Flatley, 1999) would form part of the evaluation on which future activity would be decided. Each acknowledges ignorance as a major cause of low take-up and stresses the need for more radical, focussed and targeted publicity.

The objectives of the project were described by an official involved as to "identify these people and to get them to claim ... and look at trigger points for more automatic award of benefit". 'Success' was defined as getting an 'entitled non-recipient' to receive Income Support. Entitlement would be from date of initial contact and not backdated to the date eligibility began (1997 Social Security [Claims and Payments] Regulations). The method to be used was 'data matching'; that is, matching details of claimants already held in other sections of the BA with a likely entitlement to Income Support. In the debate in the House of Commons, the Secretary of State, Harriet Harman, emphasised:

> I repeatedly pressed the Tory government to use the new computers and data matching powers not only to catch fraudsters ... but to identify pensioners who were falling through the net. (*Hansard*, 10 March 1998, col 395l)

Each participating local DSS office was supplied by BA HQ in Leeds with the names from central records of the pensioners they were to contact and the method of contact. These were to be strictly adhered to. Were it discovered, for example, that a pensioner on the list to be contacted by telephone did not have a telephone, that attempt was recorded as a 'failure' and no further attempt was made to contact them by other means. Therefore, the project was less about getting information to all older people than about methods of identifying and contacting individuals. No additional staff were taken on for the project and there was not time to train new staff. Nor were explicit targets set for increasing take-up. However, civil servants working on the project in one local office thought an 85% 'success' rate was anticipated by BA HQ by 2001/02. The local office thought that 50% was more realistic.

There is evidence of a shift in ethos and attitude to older people and rights by staff working on the projects. One senior manager commented:

> "This has priority on our time at the moment. It's a very high profile thing. It's got to be done.... Something that interests us too ... giving us a new lease of life, taken away the jaded feeling that you get at times ... a welcome change for us, giving out and looking for people to give benefits to."

Another agreed that it increased staff morale and job satisfaction and, as part of a more general trend since the change to BA, would in turn result in a better and more accountable service for customers. The emphasis on rights would also give the BA a more positive public image. The shift was summed up this way by one senior official:

"It's quite a new departure for the BA to be actually inviting, to try to identify and invite claims but it had developed from what appears to be a move within BA, obviously led by political changes. While we are independent, we carry out the policy of the current government. So to that extent political changes do affect the way we do our business ... with pensioners to an extent, it's rights more than responsibilities. They have done their bit, we ought to be paying them the benefit to which they have an entitlement.... They have a manifesto commitment in advance of the election that they wanted to do something for the poor – they have changed from the poor to the poorest pensioners.... I think it's as much to do with how they see rights and responsibilities."

The results of the pilot were expected in October 1998 (BA, 1998, p 18). However, on 17 July 1998, Harman announced in the House of Commons, as part of a debate on pensions:

we are ... going national on activity that we have been piloting.... We are introducing a new delivery system to reach something like one million forgotten pensioners. (*Hansard*, 17 July 1998, col 711)

Her announcement was described as a 'surprise' by some of those involved in the project. It had not finished and the accompanying research was neither completed nor published. Her announcement was made before an imminent government reshuffle in which it was widely expected (correctly) that she would lose her job.

The results of the pilot project were delayed and there was speculation about the reasons for the delay. Two politicians explained it this way:

"I think they [the results] have not been published. No, I bet it has not been successful, it doesn't surprise me because I can't remember a take-up campaign that was successful. Little bits of success but never anywhere near to 100%. I think there has been success in thousands of people but very rarely with elderly people do you get anywhere near."

"It depends what these little pensioner projects throw up, these pilot schemes to try and maximise, to find out why people are not claiming.... Maybe if they came forward with some blindingly original idea which could be sorted, maybe it would take some of the heat out of this. I know that the results are now known and it can't have been a huge success or we would have heard more about it."

The evaluation of the pilot projects was published more than a year late, on 14 December 1999. Overall, only 5% of 'pilot eligible' cases made a successful claim, compared to 2% of the control group (Croden et al, 1999). Uncertainty was one of the main reasons given for not claiming. The evaluation also suggested that 'data matching' is not an effective method for identifying 'eligible non-recipients' given the level of resources required. Despite high levels of political commitment, innovative activity and resources, New Labour rhetoric had not been matched by successful activity to make payments to all those older people acknowledged to be eligible.

For many, the outcome of the 'pilot' had never been in doubt. It was apparent that the government wanted to provide quick, tangible results, 'a quick win', and to be seen to be doing something in one area of social security. One senior official involved in the pilot project explained it this way:

> "From a political point of view they like to be seen to be doing things ... they have been told 'there's a million people out there, find them'.... It's what the Labour Government was elected on ... success can be achieved fairly quickly even if success is saying well actually there aren't a million people there's only 100,000 and we can prove it because we've done this ... it's probably easier to target pensioners."

Reactions to the project from officers in voluntary organisations, while welcoming the initiative, were also sceptical about New Labour's welfarist motives:

> "Inevitably the search for a certain client group to try to increase take-up, you are going to think there is something very clear behind that, isn't there, or there is going to be ... political considerations ... the pensioner group being targeted and how people respond to different groups and the point about 'deserving' and 'undeserving' poor. People don't tend to question pensioners, they are not like lone parents. People will make judgements."

> "There's a whole emphasis at the moment on old people, they are doing pilot schemes which you can see is linked to the pensioner guaranteed income because unless they can find these people it's not worth very much.... Clearly there is much more fertile ground if you are interested in maximising take-up than old people. The good news is that they are doing it. It goes back to why have they taken the decision they have to go for that group? It's a soft target politically, it gets a lot of Brownie points ... a manifesto commitment which at the time, if you are going to be simple, in terms of electioneering is quite a group that everyone is sympathetic to."

Other 'political' explanations for this high profile policy suggest a move to deflect attention from other, more controversial issues. The issue of low take-up among pensioners was part of a long-term debate both in the House and elsewhere about the future of state retirement pensions. An increasingly vocal and effective lobby of older people was pressing for change. The pilot project hoped to provide 'speedy' assistance to the poorest while the Pensions Provision Group worked on their report. One voluntary agency officer suggested:

"in terms of pensioners I think it's probably or possibly a way, they have upped income support for pensioners, a way of deflecting I imagine a debate about the level of the basic pension. It's ... popular."

Blair's speech at the 1997 Labour Party Conference had the ring of a politician speaking with conviction. It supports an explanation for the project based on enhancing the citizenship status of older people. However it is clear that 'political' explanations are also convincing. One politician was forthright in his view:

"It's really an Achilles heel politically for the government if they don't get the take-up rates up for pensioners. This is a big political problem for the government."

Minimum Income Guarantee

The whole picture of welfare benefits for the poorest pensioners became confused before the results of the pilot project were published by government talk about Minimum Income Guarantee (MIG). This had been proposed in advance of 'Partnership in Pensions' (DSS, 1998e) and was intended as a one-off increase in Income Support for pensioners. Walker (1999, p 519) was curious about its introduction:

The first striking thing about the Green Paper *Partnership in Pensions* (DSS, 1998) is the tiny amount of space devoted to today's pensioners – by any objective standard the most pressing issue that should confront a review of pensions.... The MIG is essentially a case of back to the future.... In fact the MIG is not a new benefit at all, it is income support renamed.

From April 1999, the rate of MIG for single pensioners was £75 a week, and was to be increased annually in line with earnings (DSS press release, 9 November 1999, 99/275). As a means-tested benefit, MIG had to be claimed. A high-profile launch of MIG would be expected for this more generous benefit aimed at a group to whom the government had pledged extra support. However, there was no publicity – and no application form – for 12 months after its introduction. There was plenty of confusion, for claimants and others, about a benefit sometimes referred to as Income Support and sometimes as MIG. Two politicians described the confusion thus:

"It is important really that we are going to focus most support on the poorest pensioners through the minimum income guarantee. And what is the mpg [sic]? It is simply IS up-rated quite a bit more and index linked to earnings.... Now firstly you've got to explain to people what the mpg [sic] is, the explanation must include that it's not a guarantee at all, you have to claim it,

and there's a huge information task there in terms of boosting take-up....
But it's a complicated message."

"It [MIG] was all done on the back of an envelope ... it was very confusing
for old people. Here in this place [House of Commons], even where there
are people who study these things ... there was a lot of confusion when they
were talking about everybody was going to get £75 and everybody thought
'that's great, there would be no old person would get less than £75'. It was
never thus.... It has to be claimed.... So if there was confusion here, what
happens in High Streets in the country?"

Minimum Income Guarantee appeared to be an ad hoc scheme introduced
when the pilot projects had not produced the expected results and while pension
reform was still a long way off.

Two years after the pilot project began government policy became clearer. A
major publicity campaign for MIG started in May 2000, "the biggest ever
campaign to reach pensioners who are missing out on their entitlement to
extra help" (DSS press release, 29 March 2000 00/088). The campaign was
radical. It had three strands: a free telephone call centre, a mail shot by early
November 2000 to two million potential customers "identified using advanced
data matching techniques" (BA, 2000, p 1), and television advertisements to
support the mail shot. The cost of the campaign would be £15 million, of
which just under a quarter was for publicity (some £3 million) and the remainder
for processing claims. This, like the pilot project, was not simply to be an
exercise in widely disseminating information, but a much more expensive,
proactive and individual approach. This level of resources devoted to one group
of claimants indicates their status as citizens and the importance of MIG's success:

Finding the missing pensioners has now become top priority, with Thora
Hird kicking off a TV take-up campaign next month. Research suggests it
is not pensioner pride but ignorance that stops them claiming. (Toynbee,
2000, p 21)

By February 2001, around 840,000 people had responded to the campaign.
Government estimates, however, show that take-up fell between 1998 and
2000. The drive to increase take-up continues with a simpler application
form, a freephone MIG Claim Line, leaflets, identification of key life-events
(triggers) to encourage claims and with closer links to other agencies. Although
no longer the focus of high profile announcements, there is a quiet determination
and a shift to more coherent and planned take-up work to encourage older
people to claim their entitlements. Minimum Income Guarantee will be replaced
by pensioner credit in October 2003.

Summary

The characteristics of pensioner poverty have not changed since the 1960s (although by 1997 there was increasing inequality). Cross-party rhetoric about 'deserving' older people had not changed much either. Sporadic but unsuccessful attempts to publicise these benefits raise questions about successive governments' commitment to the rights of this group. New Labour's approach, however, marked a significant change from mere rhetoric. The policy was not simply 'symbolic' (Hill, 1997), nor did presentation take precedence over innovation or substance (Ditch, 1999; Painter, 1999). On the contrary, New Labour was initially uncharacteristically quiet about the 'good news' of the more generous MIG. Although the pilot project was not 'successful' in paying benefit to many of those entitled, it was an innovative campaign that has been followed by proactive sustained information and publicity to inform older people of their entitlement.

The Prime Minister and the Chancellor expressed genuine concern for this group of older people. This was a shift in information policy that resulted in concessions to a rights agenda. However, it is clear that other explanations for this radical approach in information policy must be considered. Labour had been in opposition for 18 years. It needed policies to distance itself from the previous administration. The priority given to the pilot projects and the MIG campaign can partly be understood as an answer to the government's own need for quick and popular activity that would not harm them electorally and would honour their manifesto commitment. High level commitment ensured that administrative and financial concerns were not a major constraint on the project, although as one official involved commented, the national scheme had "to be the most cost effective at the end of the day". The involvement of the Treasury in making and implementing the policy was crucial.

This heightened activity to publicise ad hoc and stopgap policies has also to be seen as a way to deflect attention from other more controversial issues. Debates within the Labour Party on the issue of pension reform, in particular over restoring the link between state retirement pension and earnings, have so far failed to resolve the issue. Restoring the link would reduce older people's reliance on means-tested benefits and arguably diminish the need for information. Instead, and at a greater financial cost, the Chancellor introduced well-publicised additional financial help for targeted pensioners – free television licences for those aged 75+, increased winter fuel payments for all those aged 60+, and increased capital limits for MIG (DSS press release, 9 November 1999, 99/275). These were an attempt to stem criticism of a refusal to restore the link but did not succeed in deflecting the debate.

New Labour's approach has been acknowledged by politicians, civil servants and academics as a change in ethos. It also demonstrates a shift in definition of the concept of citizenship. Recognition and enhancing the citizenship status of older people by increasing their income accords with New Labour's intention of security for those who cannot, and are not expected to work. New Labour is not expecting older people to be wholly active in finding out for themselves. The government has taken active responsibility for informing them individually of their rights (although with limited success so far).

Very significantly, however, this does not improve things for those who are not entitled to means-tested benefits, for whom only an uprating of the basic retirement pension would give recognition of citizenship status to all older people. Targeting those in greatest need is a "technical solution" to the perceived problem, not "part of a universalistic welfare programme" (Higgs, 1995, p 547). This case study shows that New Labour's activity was not simply a return to 'welfarism', although there is evidence of a genuine desire to help a selected group of older people receive their benefits. That genuine desire is also seen to work in the government's political interest and helps to explain why New Labour was willing to take a radical approach to this long-standing issue.

NINE

Information for citizenship?

This book has explored government policies to promote welfare. In doing so, it has shown that this is a legitimate issue of public concern, and one that raises questions of social justice and social inclusion. Information has a central role in access to services and benefits. Assumptions that the aim of information policy is simply to facilitate access, to enable the exercise of rights and maximise take-up have been rigorously challenged. Information policy and practice have other agendas which have a direct bearing on the effectiveness of social policies and on the outcome for individuals. Attitudes to groups of claimants and to their status as citizens are reflected in policy.

Policy making has been shown here, and elsewhere in the literature, to be a complex process. It results from reconciling many often contradictory issues and pressures. The example of balancing the information needs of potential claimants with the need to contain or reduce expenditure – both administrative (including publicity) and programme costs – has long been familiar to policy makers. One politician expressed it this way:

> "There's a tension at the heart of the system, sometimes explicit, sometimes implicit, between the desire to inform people of their rights and to improve take-up, against a Treasury concern that if you were successful in that objective it would drive a coach and horses through that year, and indeed that decade's expenditure constraints. There has always been that tension there ... so that although some ministers in some eras and in some governments might be more beneficent about that, to say that they are wanting to improve take-up, and I'm sure that they truly mean it, there is this inevitable and well-known tension in the system."

Information policy mirrors the aims of those who devise, provide and administer welfare schemes. It is contingent on the priority given to the service or benefit itself. Information is necessary because of the complex structure of welfare schemes but the welfare state was built on the assumption of a less than 100% take-up.

The implications of political ideology for information policy are not clear. There are paradoxes, tensions, inconsistencies and ambivalent attitudes within each broad perspective. As discussed throughout this book, it is not possible to neatly correlate distinctive ideologies with distinctive attitudes towards information. Sometimes the results are surprising. At times when 'rights' might be thought to be a foremost concern, governments have deliberately withheld information from certain groups (for example, lone mothers in the 1960s). Conversely, there have been high level and proactive campaigns for selected benefits even when governments were aiming to reduce expenditure and discourage dependency. Thatcher's Conservative government, for example, seemed clear in its anti-welfare views but provided some effective methods of informing the public. New Labour seems unsure about whether to be tough or tender, to spend or be prudent and how far to retain a culture of secrecy. So far, the ambiguity of the Third Way has resulted in active publicity campaigns for selected 'citizens'.

The aims of welfare services as a whole, and of individual services and benefits in particular, and their role within the wider agenda are neither straightforward nor static. Therefore, information policy, in reflecting and promoting those aims and roles, will not be straightforward or static either. Social security in particular is "the stuff of politics, open to debate and fundamental disagreement" (Ditch, 1999, p 37). Policy is formulated by weighing up the strengths of often competing arguments, taking into account a lack of consensus among the public towards many provisions of the welfare state. Information policy may consequently promote or hinder claims from those who are eligible.

Promoting claims

There are examples throughout this book of government activities and campaigns motivated by a genuine desire to see more people claim the benefits to which they are entitled. They include: simplifying schemes to make it easier for claimants to understand their entitlements; providing and distributing leaflets to the public free of charge; setting up dedicated free telephone helplines to make it easier to obtain information. These can be described as 'welfarist' aims. However, as one senior official commented:

> "You should not assume that encouraging claims is one of the objects of publicity, because it was not necessarily."

Indeed, evidence has been presented throughout this book to show that there are other objectives. Some are 'political'. They can be summarised as promoting political values and goals, as enhancing political legitimacy and image, and as political pragmatism and expediency. These objectives result in activity which aims to educate the public about behaviour that fits with the wider government agenda, which provides 'good' news, and distracts attention away from 'bad' news in order to maximise electoral support and to increase the chance of policy success. 'Political' motives may also further vested interests, either promoting a particular policy for personal reasons or for career advancement.

Other reasons for policy decisions to promote benefits can be described as 'administrative' or 'organisational'. Although helpful to an understanding of how policy is made, this is not to suggest that there is necessarily a clear-cut division between these and 'political' objectives. Some administrative or organisational decisions are based on 'political' choices, while others may be independent of immediate political influence. However, they can be summarised as acting in accordance with legislation that explicitly requires information to be provided, or confers a responsibility to do so (even though this may be discretionary and imprecise), as administrative practices and operating procedures by which the information machine routinely rolls on, and as a recognition that encouraging claims for some services and benefits can save money in both the short and longer term.

It is also clear that information policy is often the outcome of a combination of issues and motives. Promoting in-work benefits, for example, furthers the government's political and re-moralising agendas by sending a clear message about the behaviour expected of citizens while, at the same time, increasing the income of families as a tangible and popular demonstration of a commitment to reduce poverty. The Minimum Income Guarantee (MIG) campaign may have been motivated by genuine personal concern for those older people not receiving their entitlements, but it happily coincides with a public concern for this 'deserving' group, thereby enhancing the government's legitimacy and popularity.

Hindering claims

It has also been evident throughout this book that decisions are taken not to mount a publicity campaign for some welfare benefits, or not to provide information above the very basic level. Steele's (1993, p 12) description of a policy of "rationing by ignorance", whether deliberate or inadvertent, contributes to an understanding of attitudes to some groups of claimants as citizens. Marsden (1973, p 276), writing about lone mothers, puts it this way: "Rights which were so inadequately publicized ... could scarcely be called rights at all".

Again, evidence points to 'political' motives. Some of these are the counterpart of those given to explain why information *is* provided. Information policy may hinder claims when it furthers political values – where promoting benefits is seen as encouraging dependence on the state rather than encouraging self-reliance. It may support the aim of a more residual welfare state or a view that actively promoting welfare is an intrusion that does not respect the individual's freedom not to claim. This perspective may also regard the promotion of benefits as encouraging abuse and fraud and of increasing discontent. Hindering claims can be politically pragmatic and expedient where the promotion of unpopular schemes is considered electorally dangerous, or to alienate public opinion, or risk a moral backlash. Claims may be hindered by a lack of agreement or interdepartmental wrangling about policy, or a lack of personal or vested interest in promoting a particular service or benefit. An uncertainty about the line between party propaganda and promotion of welfare has also been shown to be a stumbling block for information policy, as has the existence of other government priorities, either within or outside discrete areas of welfare provision.

Policy decisions *not* to promote benefits can also be described as 'administrative' or 'organisational'. As discussed earlier, legislation confers only limited responsibility on government. A reluctance to inform may stem from the belief that benefit take-up rates are adequate, that evidence of the extent of under-claiming is unreliable, and that policies are successful. It may be felt that there is sufficient information available or that benefits paid automatically do not need promoting. Bad experiences of earlier campaigns that have raised expectations or had other unexpected (negative) consequences deter information providers. There is also uncertainty about how to promote benefits and a feeling that government may not be the best or most effective provider of information.

Administrative and organisational constraints are often cited as the reason for inadequate information provision. Overstretched departments and fears of being overwhelmed by 'successful' campaigns, or failures in administrative systems and in the information machine, may result in the view that limiting the number of claims is essential for the system to work. Cost cutting has been an implicit and sometimes explicit aim of policy makers. Minimising expenditure on publicity and information, and thereby reducing demand, is a way of saving taxpayers' money and stemming the inexorable rise in the social security and other welfare budgets. When welfare is not a government priority, cuts are made to fit with the wider economic agenda. When choices have to be made, some policies never reach the information agenda. However, Donnison (1975, p 312) cautions "most important constraints ... usually appear in the guise of scarce resources".

As with policies designed to promote benefits, it is again evident that reasons for policy decisions to hinder claims can overlap. Bad experiences can serve to confirm that mounting publicity campaigns is not an effective way of increasing take-up. A perceived need to reduce programme and administrative expenditure happily ties in with a wish to reduce dependency on benefit. The relative power of each argument will change at different times and for different policies.

Inherent problems

Whatever the explanations for information policy, there have seemed over the years to be inherent problems in informing those who are eligible but not claiming their entitlements. Governments since the 1950s have admitted to failures and to continuing levels of ignorance. Campaigns that satisfy policy makers too often do not make a difference. Experience of early AIDS campaign provides a graphical illustration. Johnson (1990, p 219) observes that "all politicians have a tendency to confuse intent with accomplishment and to exaggerate their influence over events". The high level commitment of ministers can be crucial to success, but campaigns which are politically effective may be no more than symbolic, making little difference to potential claimants. There may be perverse or unanticipated results, sometimes surprising and overwhelming the administration, sometimes failing to increase take-up. The results of some campaigns – for example, to increase 'pension awareness' – may not be apparent for many years. 'Implementation deficits' (Hill, 1997) may result in failure (although implementation is itself part of policy making).

Other initiatives and campaigns have been less than successful because of the nature of the policy-making process. Information providers often have short notice of the need to publicise a benefit. The Chancellor's 'surprise' announcement of winter fuel payments in November 1997 was "a little difficult at the time" according to officials responsible for informing the public. Another senior official commented:

> "The main thing about the background to publicity is that we were horribly affected by the ad hoc-ery of politics…. Things would change very, very quickly, in politics things do change very, very quickly."

Planning and provision may be overtaken by events and by more urgent issues. Politicians move on to other more topical issues. The incremental nature of much policy making underlines the importance of departmental staff being well-informed. It also means for example that recently issued leaflets can go out of date almost as soon as they are produced, and that systems are needed to make sure that publicity and information in all outlets is up to date.

The complexity of many welfare schemes, particularly where services and benefits have to be claimed, provides another challenge for providers of information. Some observers conclude that schemes are deliberately obscure to reduce the number of claims. Others see it as an inherent problem of the way schemes evolve. One politician described it this way:

> "The system is so complicated that even if you had the best information system in the world … it would still be a problem picking your way through it and understanding it … the system has built up into a statutory edifice which nobody in the world can really understand or hope to understand."

Finding ways to provide information that is clear and concise, and that is sufficiently detailed to accurately reflect the legislation without confusing, raising expectations or misleading potential claimants, is difficult. One senior official expressed the problem as "difficult audiences, often with problems in their lives", while other observers see it more in terms of trying to sell a 'poor product'.

Other problems can be traced back to the methods chosen to inform the public. Project Access, for example (see Chapter Six of this book), which revamped all benefit leaflets, was applauded and welcomed by many, but its 'success' – and its objectives – must be questioned in the light of research into claiming behaviour. Despite providing the traditional backbone of information policy, leaflets are not an effective way of increasing take-up. Many claimants are unlikely to get information about their entitlement in this way, despite evidence that government information is crucial to the outcome for many claimants.

Nevertheless, it has been possible to overcome some of these seemingly inherent problems. Major factors are the aims and objectives of information policy and policy makers at all levels, the political will to overcome the difficulties and how the issues summarised above are reconciled in formulating information policy. Successful campaigns have increased the number of claimants of some selected benefits. There is evidence that policies to reduce or limit claims have also succeeded. Ignorance and low take-up are sometimes the result of deliberate government policy.

Information and citizenship

Citizenship is an expression of political values. 'Information for citizenship' was clear for the postwar welfare state. The government's wish for citizens to realise their newly acquired rights coincided happily with the political need for those policies to succeed. However as the real world has moved on, there have been shifts in definitions and attitudes to citizenship. Postwar social democracy aimed for participation through the exercise of rights; the New Right stressed self-reliance, choice and responsibility; the Third Way rhetoric is of responsibility and opportunity. One way in which information policy reflects shifting notions of citizenship is illustrated by the extent to which the 'information poor' are responsible for their own ignorance. Policy has moved from the paternalism of postwar labour, to the 'do-it-yourself' schemes of the 1980s, and selective personal invitations to claim at the end of the last century.

There is also evidence, reflected in information policy, of another broad and consistent shift, from an 'entitlement society' in which citizenship is by virtue of membership regardless of behaviour, to a 'contribution society' where citizenship is a reciprocal relationship (Plant, 1998). One politician expressed it this way:

> "I suppose you could argue that certainly in recent times we've seen the rise of information that is not just about telling people to claim benefit but information which is trying to balance that with, in a sense, indicating to people … how they should behave."

Resources have increasingly been focussed on promoting benefits that are clear in that aim. Since the 1970s, the agendas and values of political parties, and the economic climate, have impelled governments to promote those benefits which encourage people into work, or to stay in low-paid jobs. The emphasis on incentives to get people back into the labour market has been interpreted by King and Wickham-Jones (1999, p 277) as "a recasting of the Labour Party's notion of social citizenship. Previously the Party had adopted a version of Marshall's citizenship, based on universal and unconditional entitlement". The fact that these 'worker-citizens' remain partly dependent on social security does not diminish their status. More recent reworking by New Labour of the relationship between rights and responsibilities has made it clear that poorer older people, having already contributed to society, are also 'deserving'. Innovative and expensive policies aim to get them to claim the minimum benefit income to which their citizenship status entitles them. Case Studies A and B (Chapters Seven and Eight of this book) explored how it was possible for the rhetoric to be matched by reality. Hitherto inherent difficulties have been addressed, even if they have not been wholly successful in significantly increasing take-up rates. New Labour's language of social inclusion has resulted in many (though not enough) low-paid workers and poorer older people becoming 'information rich'.

Information provision has changed with shifting attitudes to – and definitions of – citizenship. The status of women, for example, is illustrated by publicity leaflets for the in-work benefits described in Case Study A (Chapter Seven; see also Appendix B of this book). The social security scheme was built on the assumption of the man as breadwinner and as benefit claimant. The FIS leaflet in 1971 has no picture on the cover (claims had to be made jointly and either partner could receive the benefit); the FC leaflet in 1981 pictured a two-parent family (the woman had to claim and receive the benefit); the WFTC leaflet in 1999 has on its cover a (cartoon) female (there is a choice about who claims and who receives).

This book has shown that there are better strategies for some groups and subtle mechanisms for denying information to others. The citizenship status of some other groups has sometimes been clear; for example in the virtual denial of information to 16- and 17-year-olds. Sometimes it has been ambiguous; for example, information for lone mothers to encourage them into work (which denies the value and status of caring responsibilities). Information about benefits for disabled people has fluctuated between active promotion, confusion and public threats to remove benefit from existing claimants. Questions about the status of people with disabilities vis-à-vis paid work, and about the role of social security benefits, perpetuate the social model of disability.

Social policies are used both to promote and to undermine citizenship. Welfare reform is increasingly a "tool to persuade citizens of the superiority of its [New Labour] citizenship perspective" (Dwyer, 2000, p 90). The status of those groups for whom information policy is ambiguous is not that of full citizenship. Policy is still influenced by notions of the 'deserving' and 'undeserving'. Information is a powerful tool in an unequal relationship. The explanations for promoting some benefits and not promoting others are fashioned around concepts of citizenship. This is a shift in policy from benefits for the poor simply being inherently poorly publicised and administered.

For information policy to ensure that all those with entitlements do not lose out because of ignorance more radical activity is necessary. There is no lack of ideas. There is pressure for a statutory duty to inform, pressure to develop and increase the automatic payment of benefits and to develop the use of information technology. New Labour's targets for e-government may be new, but recognition of its potential is not. The Department for Health and Social Security's (DHSS) Operational Strategy published as long ago as 1980 – "among the list of notable disasters ... which finished around £2 billion over budget but failed to deliver key project goals" (Hudson, 2002, p 523) – aimed to use new technology to provide more efficient and cheaper methods to inform claimants (Bellamy, 1996; *Hansard*, 5 March 1996, col 163) and to improve service delivery. Adler and du Feu (1974, p 68) had by then already recognised that:

> [computers are] a good deal cheaper than the cost per head of advertising individual benefits ... *whether or not it is seen as reasonable depends on the value attached to providing people with information regarding their entitlement.* (emphasis added)

Little seems to have changed.

This book has analysed the policies of promoting welfare. There is evidence of information policy that aims to enable citizens to exercise their rights, even though this often coincides with other explanations. It has also been shown that policy is heavily influenced by activity that fits with government values and goals. One politician was unequivocal in his view:

> "The politicians decide to put money into making it known, the detail of benefit entitlement, when it suits their political purposes and for no other reason."

It is clear that information policy strongly influences which claimants are able to exercise their rights. Targeting is a clear demonstration of attitudes to what it means to be – and, by implication, not to be – a citizen. In our risk society, 'information poverty', which results in many of those who are eligible not receiving their entitlements, has to be attributed in part to government policy.

References

Abel-Smith, B. (1958) 'Whose welfare state?', in N. MacKenzie (ed) *Conviction*, London: MacGibbon and Kee, pp 55-73.

Abel-Smith, B. and Townsend, P. (1965) *The poor and the poorest*, Occasional Papers on Social Administration 17, London: Bell.

Adler, M. and du Feu, D. (1974) 'Benefit from a computer', *New Society*, 10 January, pp 67-8.

Adviser (1992) No 32, London: NACAB/Shelter.

Age Concern (1998a) *Benefit take-up and older people*, Briefings 0398, London: Age Concern.

Age Concern (1998b) 'SERPS for widows/widowers from 6 April 2000', Letter to John Denham MP, London: Age Concern.

Age Concern (2000) *Debate of the age, summary of participation*, London: Age Concern.

Alcock, P. (1989) 'Why citizenship and welfare rights offer new hope for new welfare in Britain', *Critical Social Policy*, vol 26, pp 32-43.

Alcock, P. (1990) 'The end of the line for social security: the Thatcherite restructuring of welfare', *Critical Social Policy*, vol 30, pp 88-105.

Alcock, P. (1998) '2020 vision? The Green Paper on Welfare Reform', *Social Policy Association News*, May/June, pp 28-9.

Alcock, P. (1999) 'Development of social security', in J. Ditch (ed) *Introduction to social security: Policies, benefits and poverty*, London: Routledge.

Alcock, P. and Shepherd, J. (1987) 'Take-up campaigns: fighting poverty through the post', Critical *Social Policy*, vol 19, pp 52-67.

Alcock, P., Shepherd, J., Stewart, G. and Stewart, J. (1991) 'Welfare rights work into the 1990s – a changing agenda', *Journal of Social Policy*, vol 20, no 1, pp 41-63.

Allard, A., Folkard, K. and Harwood, S. (1999) *Sort it out!*, Ilford: Coalition on Young People and Social Security/Barnado's.

Allbeson, J. (1997) *Short changed*, London: NACAB.

Allen Committee Report (1965) *Committee of enquiry into the impact of rates on households*, Cmnd 2582, London: HMSO.

Atkinson, A.B. (1969) *Poverty in Britain and the reform of social security*, Cambridge: Cambridge University Press.

Atkinson, A.B. (1989) *Poverty and social security*, London: Harvester Wheatsheaf.

BA (Benefits Agency) (1991) *Framework document*, Leeds: BA.

BA (1995a) *1995/2000: A framework for the Agency* (FWD 1), London: DSS/BA.

BA (1995b) *Customer Service Report*, London: DSS/BA.

BA (1996) *Annual Report*, Leeds: BA.

BA (1997) *Benefits Agency Business Plan 1997/1998* (BPL 1), Leeds: BA.

BA (1998) *Benefits Agency Business Plan 1998/1999* (BPL 1), Leeds: BA.

BA (1999) *Customer Charter*, Cm 461, Leeds: BA.

BA (2000) *Touchbase 21: Newsletter for community organisations and professionals*, Leeds: BA.

BA Wales (1996) *Blueprint for the future*, Cardiff: BA Wales.

Bailey, L. and Pyres, J. (1996) *Communications with the Benefits Agency*, In-house Report 20, London: Analytic Services Division/DSS.

Banks, L. (1990) 'From public service to private company', *Welfare Rights Bulletin 99*, pp 2-3.

Barbalet, J.M. (1988) *Citizenship*, Milton Keynes: Open University.

Barker, D. (1971) 'The family income supplement', in D. Bull (ed) *Family poverty*, London: Duckworth/CPAG, pp 70-82.

Barnett, C. (1987) *The audit of war*, London: Macmillan.

Barrett, S. and Fudge, C. (1981) *Policy and action*, London: Methuen.

BBC (1999) 'Woman's Hour' (Radio Four), 6 January.

Bellamy, C. (1996) 'Transforming social security benefits administration for the twenty-first century: towards one-stop services and the client group principle?', *Public Administration*, vol 74, pp 159-79.

Bellamy, C. and Henderson, A. (1992) 'The UK Social Security Benefits Agency: a case study of the information polity?', *Informatization and the Public Sector*, vol 2, pp 1-26.

Bennett, F. (1987) 'What future for social security?', in A. Walker and C. Walker (eds) *The growing divide*, London: CPAG.

Berthould, R., Benson, S. and Williams, S. (1986) *Standing up for claimants*, London: Policy Studies Institute.

Beveridge, W.H. (1942) *Social insurance and allied services*, Cmd 6404, London: HMSO.

Birch, R. (1983) 'Policy analysis in the DHSS: some reflections', *Public Administration Bulletin*, vol 43, pp 18-35.

Blair, T. (1996) Speech, 25 March, in *The Guardian*, 22 June 1999, p 16.

Blair, T. (1997) Speech to Annual Labour Party Conference, Brighton, 30 September.

Blair, T. (1998) *The Third Way*, London: Fabian Society.

Bloch, A. (1993) *Access to benefits: The information needs of minority ethnic groups*, London: Policy Studies Institute.

Bochel, C. and Bochel, H. (1998) 'The governance of social policy', in E. Brunsdon, H. Dean and R. Woods (eds) *Social Policy Review 10*, London: Social Policy Association, pp 57-74.

Borrie, G. (1994) *Social justice, strategies for national renewal*, London: Vintage.

Bottomley, V. (1972) 'Families with low income in London', *Poverty*, no 22, pp 11-12.

Bradshaw, J. (1985) 'Tried and found wanting: the take-up of means-tested benefits', in S. Ward (ed) *DHSS in crisis*, London: CPAG, pp 102-11.

Briggs, E. and Rees, A.M. (1980) *Supplementary benefit and the consumer*, London: Bedford Square Press and NCVO.

Brown, G. (1999) 'Tackling the poverty trap', *The Guardian*, 7 September, p 19.

Buckland, S. and Dawson, P. (1989) 'Household claiming behaviour', *Social Policy and Administration*, vol 23, no 1, pp 60-71.

Bull, D. (1970) *Action for welfare rights*, Fabian Research Series 286, London: Fabian Society.

Bull, D. (ed) (1971) *Family poverty*, London: Duckworth/CPAG.

Bulmer, M. and Rees, A.M. (eds) (1996) *Citizenship today: The contemporary relevance of T.H. Marshall*, London: UCL Press.

Burchardt, T. and Hills, J. (1999) 'Public expenditure and the public/private mix', in M. Powell (ed) *New Labour, new welfare state? The 'third way' in British social policy*, Bristol: The Policy Press, pp 29-49.

Butcher, T. (1995) *Delivering welfare*, Buckingham: Open University.

Butler, D. and King, A. (1965) *The British General Election of 1964*, London: Macmillan.

Cabinet Office (1997) *Your right to know*, Cm 3818, London: The Stationery Office.

Cabinet Office (1998) 'Service first: the New Charter Programme' (www.servicefirst.gov.uk/1998/introduc/nine).

Charter 88 (1992) *Freedom of information*, London: Charter 88.

Citizen's Charter (1991) *Citizen's Charter*, Cm 1599, London: HMSO.

Cochrane, A. and Clarke, J. (eds) (1993) *Comparing welfare states*, Milton Keynes: Open University.

Cohen, R. and Tarpey, M. (1986) 'Are we up on take-up?', *Poverty*, no 63, pp 19-20.

Cole, D. and Utting, J. (1962) *The economic circumstances of old people*, Welwyn: Codicot Press.

Colebatch, H. (1998) *Policy*, Buckingham: Open University Press.

Cook, D. (1989) *Rich law, poor law*, Milton Keynes: Open University.

Coote, A. (ed) (1992) *The welfare of citizens*, London: Institute for Public Policy Research/Rivers Oram Press.

Corden, A. (1982) 'New light on claiming FIS: implications for take-up', *Poverty*, no 53.

Corden, A. (1995) *Changing perspectives on benefit take-up*, York: SPRU, University of York.

Corden, A. (1999) 'Claiming entitlements', in J. Ditch (ed) *Introduction to social security*, London: Routledge, pp 134-55.

Corden, A. and Craig, P. (1991) *Perceptions of family credit*, London: HMSO/ SPRU, University of York.

Costigan, P., Finch, H., Jackson, B., Legard, R. and Ritchie, J. (1999) *Overcoming barriers: Older people and income support*, DSS Research Report 100, Leeds: Corporate Document Services.

Cox, R.H. (1998) 'The consequences of welfare reform: how conceptions of social rights are changing', *Journal of Social Policy*, vol 27, no 1, pp 1-16.

CPAG (Child Poverty Action Group) (1967-74) *Poverty*, various issues, London: CPAG: no 5 (1967); no 7 (1968a); no 8 (1968b); no 10 (1969); no 15 (1970); no 29 (1974).

CPAG (nd, mid-1980s) *Benefits take-up: Facts, figures and campaign details*, London: CPAG.

CPAG (1998) *Social Security Bill briefing*, London: CPAG.

Craig, P. (1991) 'Costs and benefits: a review of research on take-up of income related benefits', *Journal of Social Policy*, vol 20, no 4, pp 537-65.

Croden, N., Costigan, P. and Whitfield, G. (1999) *Helping pensioners: Evaluation of the income support pilots*, DSS Research Report 105, London: DSS.

Crosland, C.A.R. (1964) *The future of socialism*, London: Jonathan Cape.

Crossman, R. (1977) *The diaries of a cabinet minister*, vol 3, London: Hamish Hamilton and Jonathan Cape.

Cummins, J. (1996) *National customer survey*, Leeds: BA.

Cummins, J. and Spilsbury, M. (1998) 'The demand for information on benefits', *Benefits*, Issue 21, January, p 20.

Curran, C. (1960) *Forward from Beveridge*, London: Crossbow.

Daniel, C. (1998) 'Radical, angry and willing to work', *New Statesman*, 6 March, pp 22-3.

Dawson, P., Buckland, S. and Gilbert, N. (1990) 'Expert systems in the public provision of welfare benefit advice', *Policy & Politics*, vol 18, no 1, pp 43-54.

de Schweinitz, K. (1961) *England's road to social security*, New York: Barnes.

Deacon, A. (1982) 'An end to the means test? Social security and the Attlee government', *Journal of Social Policy*, vol 11, no 3, pp 289-306.

Deacon, A. and Bradshaw, J. (1983) *Reserved for the poor*, Oxford: Blackwell and Robertson.

Deakin, N. (1994) 'Accentuating the apostrophe: the Citizen's Charter', *Policy Studies*, vol 15, no 3, pp 48-58.

Deakin, N. and Parry, R. (1998) 'The Treasury and New Labour's social policy', in E. Brunsden, H. Dean and R. Woods (eds) *Social Policy Review 10*, London: Social Policy Association, pp 34-56.

Deakin, N. and Parry, R. (2000) *The Treasury and social policy*, London: Macmillan.

Dean, H. (1991) *Social security and social control*, London: Routledge.

Dean, H. (1999) 'Citizenship', in M. Powell (ed) *New Labour, new welfare state? The 'third way' in British social policy*, Bristol: The Policy Press, pp 213-33.

Dean, H. (2000) 'Managing risk by controlling behaviour: social security administration and the erosion of welfare citizenship', in P. Taylor-Gooby (ed) *Risk, trust and welfare*, London: Macmillan, pp 51-68.

DfEE/DSS (Department for Education and Employment/Department of Social Security) (1998) *A new contract for welfare: The gateway to work*, Cm 4102, London: The Stationery Office.

DHSS (Department of Health and Social Security) (1978) *Then and now. Thirty years of social security* (FB3), London: DHSS.

DHSS (1982-88) *Annual Reports*, 1982 (Cmnd 8494); 1983 (Cmnd 8789); 1985 (Cmnd 9428); 1987 (Cm 56); 1988(Cm 288); London: DHSS.

Ditch, J. (1993) 'Next steps', in R. Page and N. Deakin (eds) *The cost of welfare*, Aldershot: Avebury.

Ditch, J. (ed) (1999) *Introduction to social security: Policies, benefits and poverty*, London: Routledge.

Donnison, D. (1975) *Social policy and administration revisited*, London: Allen & Unwin.

Donnison, D. (1982) *The politics of poverty*, Oxford: Martin Robertson.

Doyal, L. and Gough, I. (1991) *A theory of human needs*, London: Macmillan.

Drake, R. (1999) *Understanding disability policies*, London: Macmillan.

Drewery, G. and Butcher, T. (1991) *The civil service today*, Oxford: Blackwell.

DSS (Department of Social Security) (1989-98) *Departmental Reports*, 1989 (Cm 615); 1990 (Cm 1014); 1991a (Cm1514); 1992 (Cm1914); 1993 (Cm 2213); 1994 (Cm 2513); 1995 (Cm 2813); 1996 (Cm 3213); 1997a (Cm 3613); 1998a (Cm 3913); 1999 (Cm 4212); 2000a (Cm 4614); London: HMSO/The Stationery Office.

DSS (1991b) *Family credit campaign guide*, London: DSS.

DSS (1997b) *Income-related benefits: Estimates of take-up in 1995/96*, London: DSS.

DSS (1998b) *Setting up social security* (www.dss.gov.uk/50years/poster2).

DSS (1998c) *A new contract for welfare: Principles into practice*, Cm 4101, London: The Stationery Office.

DSS (1998d) *Beating fraud is everyone's business: Securing the future*, Cm 4012, London: The Stationery Office.

DSS (1998e) *Partnership in pensions*, Cm 4179, London: The Stationery Office.

DSS (2000b) *The changing welfare state: Pensioner Incomes*, no 2, London: DSS.

DSS (2000c) *The changing welfare state: Social security spending*, London: DSS.

DSS (2000d) *Inherited SERPS statement to the House of Commons*, 15 March, London: DSS.

Dwyer, P. (2000) *Welfare rights and responsibilities*, Bristol: The Policy Press.

EC (European Commission) (1997) *Building the European information society for us all*, Luxembourg: Office for the Official Publications of the European Communities.

Elliot, L., White, M. and Brindle, D. (1997) 'Busy trying to colonise the DSS', *The Guardian*, 21 October, p 11.

Esping-Andersen, G. (1990) *The three worlds of welfare capitalism*, Cambridge: Polity Press.

Fairclough, N. (2000) *New Labour new language?*, London: Routledge.

Field, F. (1973) 'Running out of excuses', *Poverty*, no 6, pp 3-4.

Field, F. (1974) 'An anti-poverty programme for Britain – a five-year plan', *Poverty*, no 29, pp 2-5.

Field, F. (1975) 'The lost benefits', *New Society*, 27 March, p 790.

Flatley, J. (1999) *Helping pensioners: Contextual survey of the income support pilots*, In-house Report 60, London: Analytical Services Division/DSS.

Forrest, R. and Murie, A. (1991) *Selling the welfare state*, London: Routledge.

Foster, P. (1983) *Access to welfare*, London: Macmillan.

Fowler, N. (1991) *Ministers decide*, London: Chapmans.

Fraser, D. (1984) *Evolution of the British welfare state*, Basingstoke: Macmillan.

Fry, V. and Stark, G. (1987) 'The take-up of Supplementary Benefit: gaps in the safety net?', *Fiscal Studies*, vol 8, no 4, pp 1-14.

Galligan, D. (1992) 'Procedural rights in social welfare', in A. Coote (ed) *The welfare of citizens*, London: Institute for Public Policy Research/Rivers Oram Press, pp 55-68.

Garnham, A. and Knights, E. (1993) *Child support handbook*, London: CPAG.

Giddens, A. (1998) 'After the left's paralysis', *New Statesman*, 1 May, pp 18-21.

Ginn, J. and Arber, S. (2000) 'Personal pension take-up in the 1990s in relation to position in the labour market', *Journal of Social Policy*, vol 29, no 2, pp 205-28.

Glennerster, H. (1962) *National assistance: Service or charity?*, Young Fabian Pamphlet 4, London: Fabian Society.

Golding, P. and Middleton, S. (1982) *Images of welfare*, Oxford: Blackwell and Robertson.

Gore, P. (1999) 'Freedom of information under Blair', *Talking Politics*, vol 12, no 1, pp 216-21.

Green Paper (1985a) *Reform of Social Security programme for change*, Cmnd 9517 (Fowler Reforms), London: HMSO.

Green Paper (1985b) *Reform of Social Security programme for change*, Cmnd 9518 (Fowler Reforms), London: HMSO.

Green Paper (1998) *New ambitions for our country: A new contract for welfare*, Cm 3085, London: The Stationery Office.

Greenaway, J. (1998) 'The citizenship debate and British politics', *Talking Politics*, vol 10, no 3, pp 179-83.

Greer, P. (1994) *Transforming central government*, Buckingham: Open University, p 1.

Gunsteren, H.R. (1998) *A theory of citizenship: Organising plurality in contemporary democracies*, Oxford: Westview Press.

Hadwen, R. (1997) 'Saving changes', *Adviser*, no 62, pp 11-14.

Hall, P. (1963) *The social services of modern England*, London: Routledge and Kegan Paul.

Hall, P., Land, H., Parker, R. and Webb, A. (1975) *Change, choice and conflict in social policy*, London: Heineman.

Heclo, H. (1972) 'Review article: policy analysis', *British Journal of Political Science*, vol 2, no 1, pp 83-108.

Heclo, H. and Wildavsky, A. (1974) *The private government of public money*, London: Macmillan.

Hetherington, P. (1998) 'Survey of services backfires on ministers', *The Guardian*, 26 October, p 3.

Hewitt, M. (1999) 'New Labour and social security', in M. Powell (ed) *New Labour, new welfare state? The 'third way' in British social policy*, Bristol: The Policy Press, pp 149-70.

Heywood, A. (1992) *Political ideologies*, London: Macmillan.

Higgs, P. (1995) 'Citizenship and old age: the end of the road?', *Ageing and society*, vol 15, pp 535-50.

Hill, M. (1976) *The state, administration and the individual*, London: Fontana.

Hill, M. (1990) *Social security policy in Britain*, Aldershot: Edward Elgar.

Hill, M. (1993) *The policy process in the modern capitalist state*, Hemel Hempstead: Harvester Wheatsheaf.

Hill, M. (1997) *The policy process in the modern state*, London: Prentice Hall/ Harvester Wheatsheaf.

HM Treasury (1998) *Departmental Report of the Chancellor of the Exchequer's Departments*, Cm 3719, London: The Stationery Office.

HM Treasury (1999) *Departmental Report of the Chancellor of the Exchequer's Departments*, Cm 4218, London: The Stationery Office.

Home Office (1994) *Code of practice on access to government information*, London: HMSO.

Home Office (1999) *Freedom of information consultation document*, Cm 4355, London: Home Office.

Howe, L. (1985) 'The "deserving" and the "undeserving": practice in an urban, local social security office', *Journal of Social Policy*, vol 14, no 1, pp 49-72.

Hudson, J. (2002) 'Digitising the structures of government: the UK's information age government agenda', *Policy & Politics*, vol 30, no 4, pp 515-31.

Hughes, G. (1998) *Imagining welfare futures*, Milton Keynes: Open University.

Hughes, K. and Moore, N. (1993) *The role of information in the economy and society: An overview*, London: Policy Studies Institute.

IR (Inland Revenue) (1999) *Credit where it's due: An introduction to tax credits* (Videotape), London: IR.

IR (2000) *WFTC and FC statistics quarterly enquiry*, November (1999); February (2000); May (2000); London: Government Statistical Service.

Jacobs, J. (1994) 'The scroungers who never were: the effects of the 1989 Social Security Act', in R. Page and J. Baldock (eds) *Social Policy Review 6*, London: Social Policy Association, pp 126-45.

Johnson, N. (1990) *Reconstructing the welfare state*, London: Harvester Wheatsheaf.

Johnson, P. and Falkingham, J. (1992) *Ageing and economic welfare*, London: Sage Publications.

Jones, M.G. (1985) 'Citizens' rights to information: the role of government', *Information Services and Use*, vol 5, pp 37-47.

Jordan, B. (1974) *Poor parents*, London: Routledge and Kegan Paul.

Jordan, B. (1998) *The politics of welfare*, London: Sage Publications.

Joseph, K. and Sumption, J. (1979) *Equality*, London: John Murray.

Kearns, K. (1997) 'Social democratic perspectives on the welfare state', in M. Lavalette and A. Pratt (eds) *Social policy*, London: Sage Publications.

Kerr, S. (1982) 'Deciding about supplementary pensions: a provisional model', *Journal of Social Policy*, vol 11, no 4, pp 505-17.

King, D. and Waldron, J. (1988) 'Citizenship, social citizenship and the defence of welfare provision', *British Journal of Political Science*, vol 18, pp 415-43.

King, D. and Wickham-Jones, M. (1999) 'Bridging the Atlantic: the democratic origins of welfare to work', in M. Powell (ed) *New Labour, new welfare state? The 'third way' in British social policy*, Bristol: The Policy Press, pp 257-80.

Kymlicka, W. and Norman, W. (1994) 'Return of the citizen: a survey of recent work on citizenship theory', *Ethics*, vol 104, pp 352-81.

Labour Party (1997a) *Manifesto: New Labour because Britain deserves better*, London: The Labour Party.

Labour Party (1997b) *Agenda for 96th Conference*, Motion 62.

Laurance, J. (1987a) 'Frozen to death', *New Society*, 16 January, pp 18-20.

Laurance, J. (1987b) 'Avoidance tactics?', *New Society*, 29 May, pp 23-4.

Leaper, R. (1979) 'Social assistance: a watershed?', *Social Policy and Administration*, vol 13, no 1, pp 3-21.

Leaper, R. (1991) 'Introduction to the Beveridge Report', *Social Policy and Administration*, vol 25, no 1, pp 3-13.

Levin, P. (1997) *Making social policy*, Buckingham: Open University Press.

Lindblom, C. (1979) 'Still muddling, not yet through', *Public Administration Review*, November/December, pp 517-25.

Lindblom, C. (1980) *The policy making process*, New Jersey: Prentice Hall.

Ling, T. (1994) 'The new managerialism and social security', in J. Clarke, A. Cochrane and E. McLaughlin (eds) *Managing social policy*, London: Sage Publications, pp 32-56.

Lipsky, M. (1980) *Street level bureaucracy*, New York, NY: Russell Sage Foundation.

Lister, R. (1976) 'Take up: the same old story', *Poverty*, no 34, pp 3-7.

Lister, R. (1990) *The exclusive society: Citizenship and the poor*, London: CPAG.

Lister, R. (1997) *Citizenship: Feminist perspectives*, London: Macmillan.

Lister, R. (1998a) 'From equality to social exclusion: New Labour and the welfare state', *Critical Social Policy*, vol 55, pp 215-25.

Lister, R. (1998b) 'Vocabularies of citizenship and gender: the UK', *Critical Social Policy*, vol 56, pp 309-31.

Lorant, J. (1980) *The problem of take-up* (*Poverty*, Pamphlet 49), London: CPAG.

Lowe, R. (1990) 'The Second World War, consensus, and the foundation of the welfare state', *Twentieth Century British History*, vol 1, no 2, pp 152-82.

Lukes, S. (1974) *Power: A radical view*, London: Macmillan.

Lund, B. (1999) 'Ask not what your community can do for you: obligations, New Labour and welfare reform', *Critical Social Policy*, vol 61, pp 447-62.

Lynes, T. (1972) 'Welfare men', *New Society*, 14 September, pp 505-6.

Lynes, T. (1991) 'Drumming up new business', *Community Care*, 11 July, p 9.

Malpass, P. and Murie, A. (1994) *Housing policy and practice*, London: Macmillan.

Margetts, H. and Dunleavy, P. (2002) 'Cultural barriers to e-government', (Academic Article HC 704-III in Support of National Audit Office, *Better Public Services through e-government*), London: The Stationery Office.

Marinetto, M. (1999) *Studies of the policy process*, London: Prentice Hall.

Marsden, D. (1969) *Mothers alone*, London: Allen Lane/Penguin.

Marsden, D. (1973) *Mothers alone* (revised edn), London: Penguin.

Marshall, T.H. (1963) *Sociology at the crossroads*, London: Heineman.

Marshall, T.H. (1965) 'The right to welfare', *Sociological Review*, vol 13, pp 261-72.

Marshall, T.H. (1967) *Social policy in the twentieth century*, London: Hutchinson.

Marshall, T.H. (1981) *The right to welfare*, London: Heineman.

Mead, L. (1986) *Beyond entitlement*, New York, NY: Free Press.

Millar, J., Cooke, K. and McLaughlin, E. (1989) 'The employment lottery: risk and social security benefits', *Policy & Politics*, vol 17, pp 75-81.

Miller, D., Kitzinger, J., Williams, K. and Beharrell, P. (1998) *The circuit of mass communication* (Glasgow Media Group), London: Sage Publications.

Miller, S. and Perroni, F. (1992) 'Social politics and the Citizen's Charter', in N. Manning and R. Page (eds) *Social Policy Review 4*, London: Social Policy Association, pp 242-60.

Moodie, M. et al (1988) *The business of service: The report of the regional organisation scrutiny*, London: DSS.

Moore, N. (1994) 'Information policy research priorities for Europe', *Policy Studies*, vol 15, no 1, pp 16-25.

Moore, N. (1995) *Access to information – A review of the provision of disability information*, London: Policy Studies Institute.

Moore, N. (nd) 'Rights and responsibilities in an information society', Press release, London: Policy Studies Institute.

Moore, N. and Steele, J. (1991) *Information intensive Britain*, London: Policy Studies Institute.

MPNI (Ministry of Pensions and National Insurance) (1966) *Financial and other circumstances of retirement pensioners*, London: HMSO.

MSS (Ministry of Social Security) (1968a) *Note for minister. Working party on public awareness of social service benefits*, 30 July London: Public Record Office, BN 72/40.

MSS (1968b) *The consumer side of benefits*, Cmnd 3638, vol 5 (2), memo 99, London: HMSO

NACAB (National Association of Citizens' Advice Bureaux) (nd) *The inside story*, London: NACAB.

NACAB (1997) *Information society – Motion for the adjournment of the House*, London: NACAB.

NAO (National Audit Office) (1988) *Department of Health and Social Security: Quality of service to the public at local offices*, House of Commons Paper 451, London: HMSO.

NAO (1998) *Benefits Agency: Performance measurement*, House of Commons Paper 952, London: HMSO.

NAO (2000) *Supplementary report to the Permanent Secretary of the DSS* (www.dss.gov.uk/hq/pubs/serps/lessons).

NAO (2002) *Better public services through e-government* (HC 704-I), London: The Stationery Office.

NAB (National Assistance Board) (nd) *Memo re Leaflet NI 49A*, London: Public Record Office, BN 10/27.

National Assistance Board (1948-65) *Annual Reports*, 1948 (Cmd 7767); 1949 (Cmd 8030); 1950 (Cmd 8276); 1956 (Cmnd 181); 1957 (Cmnd 444); 1959 (Cmnd 1085); 1960 (Cmnd 1410); 1962 (Cmnd 2078); 1963 (Cmnd 2386); 1964 (Cmnd 2674); 1965 (Cmnd 3042).

NCC (National Consumer Council) (1977) *The fourth right of citizenship*, London: NCC.

Norton-Taylor, R. (2000) 'Matching personal data to "risk to privacy"', *The Guardian*, 10 August, p 19.

NPC (National Pensioners Convention) (1999) *The unwanted generation*, London: NPC.

Oliver, M. (1990) *The politics of disablement*, London: Macmillan.

Painter, C. (1999) 'Public service reform from Thatcher to Blair: a third way', *Parliamentary Affairs*, vol 52, no 1, pp 94-112.

Parker, J. (1975) *Social policy and citizenship*, London: Macmillan.

Parry, G. and Morriss, P. (1974) 'When is a decision not a decision?', in I. Crewe (ed) *British Political Sociology Year Book*, vol 1, London: Croom Helm, pp 317-36.

Perkins, E., Roberts, S. and Moore, N. (1991) *Helping clients claim their benefits*, London: Policy Studies Institute.

Phillips Committee (1954) *Report of the Committee on the economic and financial problems of the provision for old age*, Cmd 9333, London: HMSO.

Phillipson, C. (1981) *Capitalism and the construction of old age*, London: Macmillan.

Piven, F. and Cloward, R. (1972) *Regulating the poor*, London: Tavistock.

Plant, R. (1988a) *Citizenship, rights and socialism*, Fabian Tract 531, London: Fabian Society.

Plant, R. (1988b) 'Citizenship and society', *New Socialist*, December, pp 7-9.

Plant, R. (1992) 'Citizenship, rights and welfare', in A. Coote (ed) *The welfare of citizens: Developing new social rights*, London: Institute for Public Policy Research/ Rivers Oram Press, pp 15-29.

Plant, R. (1998) 'So you want to be a citizen?', *New Statesman*, 6 February, pp 30-2.

Poster, M. (1990) *The mode of information*, Cambridge: Polity Press.

Powell, M. (2000) 'New Labour and the Third Way in the British welfare state: a new distinctive approach?', *Critical Social Policy*, vol 62, pp 39-60.

Powell, M. (ed) (1999) *New Labour, new welfare state? The 'third way' in British social policy*, Bristol: The Policy Press.

Powell, M. and Hewitt, M. (1998) 'The end of the welfare state?', *Social Policy and Administration*, vol 32, no 1, pp 1-13.

Prottas, J.M. (1979) *People processing*, Lexington, MA: D.C. Heath.

Raab, C. (1994) 'Open government: policy information and information policy', *Political Quarterly*, vol 65, pp 340-7.

Rees, A.M. (1995a) 'The promise of social citizenship', *Policy & Politics*, vol 23, pp 313-25.

Rees, A.M. (1995b) 'The other T.H. Marshall', *Journal of Social Policy*, vol 24, no 3, pp 341-62.

Roche, M. (1992) *Rethinking citizenship*, Cambridge: Polity Press.

Rowe, M. (1999) 'Joined up accountability: bringing the citizen back in', *Public Policy and Administration*, vol 14, no 2, pp 91-102.

Sainsbury, R. (1998) 'Lost opportunities: benefit decision-making and the 1988 Social Security Act', in E. Brunsdon, H. Dean and R. Woods (eds) *Social Policy Review 10*, London: Social Policy Association, pp 123-36.

Sainsbury, R. (1999) 'The aims of social security', in J. Ditch (ed) *Introduction to social security*, London: Routledge, pp 34-47.

Seldon, A. (1977) *Charge*, London: Temple Smith.

Sharron, H. (1982) 'Post and deliver', *Social Work Today*, vol 14, no 14, 7 December, pp 8-10.

Silverstein, N. (1984) 'Informing the elderly about public services', *Gerontologist*, vol 24, no 1, pp 37-40.

Simkins, J. and Tickner, V. (1978) *Whose benefit?*, London: The Economic Intelligence Unit Limited.

SSAC (Social Security Advisory Committee) (1982) *First report of the SSAC*, London: HMSO.

SSAC (1997) *Eleventh report of the SSAC*, London: The Stationery Office.

SSC (Social Security Committee) (1998) *First report, tax and benefits: Implementation of tax credits*, House of Commons Paper 29, 25 November, London: The Stationery Office.

SSC (1999) *Second special report, tax and benefits: Implementation of tax credits*, House of Commons Paper 176, 25 January, London: The Stationery Office.

Social Security Statistics, London: HMSO.

Social Trends 1976; 1991; 1993; 1998; 2002; London: HMSO.

Spicker, P. (1993) *Poverty and social security*, London: Routledge.

Stacpoole, J. (1972) 'Running FIS', *New Society*, 13 January, pp 64-6.

Stafford, B., Walker, R., Hull, L. and Horsley, E. (1996) *Customer contact and communication with the Benefits Agency: Literature review*, In-house Report 17, London: Analytic Services Division/DSS.

Stanton, D. (1977) 'The take-up debate on the UK Family Income Supplement', *Policy & Politics*, vol 5, pp 27-45.

Steele, J. (1991) 'Information for citizens', *Policy Studies*, vol 12, no 3, pp 47-55.

Steele, J. (1993) *Informing people about social services*, London: Policy Studies Institute.

Steele, J. (1996) 'Information for users of community care services', *Assignation*, vol 14, no 1, October, pp 15-20.

Steele, J. (1997) *Information for citizenship in Europe*, London: Policy Studies Institute.

Stonefrost, M. (1990) *Encouraging citizenship*, London: HMSO.

Strauss, R. (1977) 'Information and participation in a public transfer program', *Journal of Public Economics*, vol 8, pp 385-96.

Sullivan, M. (1996) *The development of the British welfare state*, London: Prentice Hall/Harvester Wheatsheaf.

Sullivan, M. (1998) 'The social democratic perspective', in P. Alcock, A. Erskine and M. May (eds) *The student's companion to social policy*, Oxford: Blackwell/ Social Policy Association, pp 71-7.

Supplementary Benefits Commission (1975) *Annual Report*, Cmnd 6615, London: HMSO.

Supplementary Benefits Commission/DHSS (1970) *Supplementary Benefits Handbook*, London: HMSO.

Taylor, D. (1989) 'Citizenship and social power', *Critical Social Policy*, vol 26, pp 19-31.

Taylor, D. (1996) 'Citizenship, needs and participation', in D. Taylor (ed) *Critical social policy – A reader*, London: Sage Publications, pp 149-55.

Taylor-Gooby, P. (ed) (2000) *Risk, trust and welfare*, London: Macmillan.

Tester, S. and Meredith, B. (1987) *Ill-informed?*, London: Policy Studies Institute.

Times (1948) 'Leader', 5 July.

Timmins, N. (1995) *The five giants: A biography of the welfare state*, London: Harper Collins.

Tinker, A., McCreadie, C. and Salvage, A. (1993) *The information needs of elderly people*, London: Age Concern.

Titmuss, R. (1987) 'Welfare rights, law and discretion', in B. Abel-Smith and K. Titmuss (eds) *The philosophy of welfare*, London: Allen & Unwin.

Townsend, P. (1963) *The family life of old people*, London: Penguin.

Townsend, P. (1979) *Poverty in the United Kingdom*, London: Penguin.

Townsend, P. and Wedderburn, D. (1965) *The aged and the welfare state*, London: Bell.

Toynbee, P. (1998) 'Single mothers don't inhabit Fairy Liquid ads. So lets get real', *The Guardian*, 11 May, p 14.

Toynbee, P. (2000) 'Showing age concern', *The Guardian*, 7 April, p 21.

Turner, B. (1990) 'Outline of a theory of citizenship', *Sociology*, vol 24, no 2, pp 189-217.

Twine, F. (1994) *Citizenship and social rights*, London: Sage Publications.

UN (United Nations) (1996) *The Commmittee on Economic, Social and Cultural Rights: Fact sheet 16* (Revision 1), New York: UN Centre for Human Rights.

van Oorschot, W. (1991) 'Non-take-up of social security benefits in Europe', *Journal of European Social Policy*, vol 1, no 1, pp 15-30.

Victor, C.R. (1986) 'How effective are benefits take-up campaigns with elderly people?', in C. Phillipson, M. Bernard and P. Strang (eds) *Dependency and interdependency in old age: Theoretical perspectives and policy alternatives*, Beckenham: Croom Helm, pp 198-216.

Vincent, J., Leeming, A., Pecker, A. and Walker, R. (1995) *Choosing advice on benefits*, DSS Research Report 35, London: HMSO.

Walker, A. (1998) 'Older people', in P. Alcock, A. Erskine and M. May (eds) *The student's companion to social policy*, Oxford: Blackwell/Social Policy Association, pp 249-56.

Walker, A. (1999) 'The third way for pensioners (by way of Thatcherism and avoiding today's pensioners)', *Critical Social Policy*, vol 61, pp 511-27.

Walker, A. and Walker, C. (1987) *The growing divide*, London: CPAG.

Walker, C. (1982) 'The reform of the supplementary benefits scheme: for whose benefit?', in S. Jones and J. Stevenson (eds) *Yearbook of social policy in Britain*, London: Routledge and Kegan Paul, pp 179-200.

Walker, C. (1986) 'Reforming Supplementary Benefit: the impact on claimants', *Social Policy and Administration*, vol 20, no 2, pp 91-102.

Walker, R. and Brittain, K. (1995) *Benefits Agency customers and the 1994 Review of the benefits system*, In-house Report 7, London: Analytic Services Division/DSS.

Watson, S. (1998) 'New orders, disorders and creative chaos: the information age and the network society', *Policy & Politics*, vol 26, no 2, pp 227-33.

Weale, A. (1983) *Political theory and social policy*, London: Macmillan.

Webb, S. (1975) 'The abolition of National Assistance', in P. Hall, H. Land, R. Parker and A. Webb (eds) *Change, choice and conflict in social policy*, London: Heinemann.

Webster, L. (1998) 'Claims onus', *Adviser*, no 67, pp 16-18.

Welfare Rights Bulletin, 1988 (June); 1995 (124); 1996a (133); 1996b (134), London: CPAG.

Williams, F. (1999) 'Good-enough principles for welfare', *Journal of Social Policy*, vol 28, no 4, pp 667-87.

Williams, T., Astin, M. and Ditch, J. (1995*) First-time customers*, DSS Research Report 36, London: HMSO.

Wilson, J. (1996) 'Citizen Major? The rationale and impact of the Citizen's Charter', *Public Policy and Administration*, vol 11, no 1, pp 45-62.

Wilson, M. (1997) 'Citizenship and welfare', in M. Lavalette and A. Pratt (eds) *Social Policy*, London: Sage Publications, pp 182-95.

Government expenditure on publicity for social security benefits (1973-98/99)

Year	Expenditure (£)
1973	357,000[a]
1974	384,000[a]
1975	342,000[a]
1976	346,000[a]
1980	445,800[a]
1988/89	12.8 million
1989/90	13.9 million
1990/91	14.6 million
1991/92	18.0 million
1992/93	18.0 million
1993/94	10.5 million (includes 3.5 million BA expenditure)
1994/95	14.9 million (includes 5.9 million BA expenditure)[b]
1995/96	18.5 million (includes 5.9 million BA expenditure)[b]
1996/97	13.4 million (includes 4.8 million BA expenditure)[b]
1997/98	8.2 million (includes 4.2 million BA expenditure)[b]
1998/99	3.6 million (only BA figure available)[b]

Sources: [a] Hansard; [b] correspondence with the Benefits Agency (BA). All remaining figures are from government expenditure plans

Prior to 1993/94 the publicity budget was decided on a departmental basis.

Figures in *Hansard* (5 March 1996, col 163) in response to a parliamentary question about total spending by the DSS on advertising gave different figures to those above:

1993/94	5.9 million
1994/95	3.6 million
1995/96	4.4 million (estimated)

Sample leaflets and posters

[Please note that the quality of the leaflets reproduced in this Appendix was unable to be improved from their original state.]

Source: MSS (1968) 'The short step', DW 9309

...to claim your rights

This is a message to the less well-off families in Britain. Those who could more easily make ends meet by taking up the benefits which are theirs by right. **Those who are working**, as well as those who are out of a job or retired. It has nothing to do with charity. The benefits come from taxes: and everyone pays taxes in one form or another.

There is a whole range of benefits available to help people who need them—from welfare foods to rate rebates. But many people who need help, who are entitled to help, are not getting it—just because they do not claim it. It's often because people just do not know what they have to do or where they have to go to get help.

The purpose of this leaflet is to clear up any confusion. **Remember: this is not charity but your right.**

Perhaps you yourself are not in any need. But the chances are that you know someone who is. Be a good neighbour and help them take that step.

The benefits available are set out overleaf. Because no hard and fast income level applies many people are uncertain whether they qualify. **What is low income? This example may help you:** a family with 3 children aged 4, 8, and 12, with rent and rates adding up to £2 10s, and a total family income (before deduction of tax, etc.) of £14 3s, are entitled to a number of the benefits. In some cases the limit would be higher.

The officers of the Ministry of Social Security or your local council can help you to understand the rules.

You should have ....

Welfare Foods: free milk (dried or liquid) is available for expectant mothers, nursing mothers, children up to 5 years old and certain handicapped children up to 16 in families whose income is low. Expectant mothers, nursing mothers, and children up to 5 in low-income families may also be able to obtain free certain of the following: orange juice, cod-liver oil and vitamin tablets. Any family, **whatever its income**, where more than two are entitled to cheap milk is automatically entitled to free milk for all but two of them.

Free School Meals: for children if family income is low. Large families, **whatever their income**, will not have to pay for school meals for their fourth and subsequent dependent children.

Clothing for school children: free or for a small charge.

School uniforms: a small grant may be made in England and Wales towards the cost of school uniforms. If a child stays on at school after 15 he or she may be eligible for an educational maintenance allowance (in Scotland, a higher school bursary).

Medical charges: if you have to pay National Health Service charges for glasses, dentures or dental treatment you may be able to get a special grant.

Many of you are exempt from payment of prescription charges. If you have to pay a charge you may be able to obtain a refund.

ALL YOU NEED TO DO IS TO TAKE ONE SHORT STEP .... AND ASK

Source: DHSS (1982) 'Need more money?', SB 21

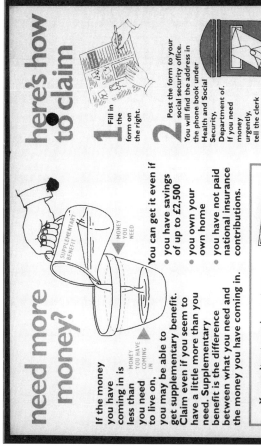

need more money?

If the money you have coming in is less than you need to live on, you may be able to get supplementary benefit. Claim even if you seem to have a little more than you need. Supplementary benefit is the difference between what you need and the money you have coming in.

You can get it even if

- you have savings of up to £2,500
- you own your own home
- you have not paid national insurance contributions.

You can't get supplementary benefit if you are in full-time work. But if you have children, you may be able to claim Family Income Supplement instead. Get this leaflet from a post office or social security office.

You may be able to get help with your rent and rates. Ask at your council offices.

here's how to claim

1 Fill in the form on the right.

2 Post the form to your social security office. You will find the address in the phone book under Health and Social Security, Department of. If you need money urgently, tell the clerk at the office.

3 You will have a talk with someone from the office to find out whether you can get supplementary benefit. The office will tell you when this will be.

147

DEPARTMENT OF HEALTH AND SOCIAL SECURITY

LEAFLET FIS 1
MAY 1971

FAMILY INCOME SUPPLEMENT: FOR FAMILIES WITH CHILDREN

Source: DHSS (1971) 'Family Income Supplement: for families with children', FIS 1

Source: DHSS (1981) 'Family Income Supplement: how to claim extra money if you're bringing up children on low earnings', FIS 1

Source: IR (1999) 'Working Families Tax Credit', WFTC/BK 1

Source: NAB (1964) 'Twenty questions':Allowances to pensioners and other elderly people',AL 51

Source: DHSS (nd) 'Cash benefit for pensioners', SB 29

Index

Also available from The Policy Press

Understanding social security

Issues for policy and practice

Jane Millar, Department of Social and Policy Sciences, University of Bath

Paperback £17.99 ISBN 1 86134 419 8
Hardback $50.00 ISBN 1 86134 420 1
240 x 172mm 360 pages May 2003

Understanding the finance of welfare

What welfare costs and how to pay for it

Howard Glennerster, London School of Economics and Political Science

Paperback £17.99 ISBN 1 86134 405 8
Hardback $50.00 ISBN 1 86134 406 6
240 x 172mm 256 pages May 2003

Welfare rights and responsibilities

Contesting social citizenship

Peter Dwyer, Department of Sociology and Social Policy, University of Leeds

Paperback £17.99 ISBN 1 86134 405 8
234 x 156mm 264 pages September 2000